My Life
Including
Prison

My Life
Including
Prison

EILEEN PRUETT

Copyright © 2021 by Eileen Pruett.

All rights reserved. No part of this publication may be reproduced, distributed, or transmitted in any form or by any means, including photocopying, recording, or other electronic or mechanical methods, without the prior written permission of the author, except in the case of brief quotations embodied in critical reviews and certain other noncommercial uses permitted by copyright law.

Printed in the United States of America
ISBN 978-1-947352-77-3 (sc)
ISBN 978-1-641336-38-3 (hc)
ISBN 978-1-641336-39-0 (e)

Library of Congress Control Number: 2021905703

Biography/Autobiography
2021.04.08

MainSpring Books
5901 W. Century Blvd
Suite 750
Los Angeles, CA, US, 90045

www.mainspringbooks.com

PROLOGUE

This book has two story lines that eventually intersect. One story is about the life I lived and the other story is about my experience working as a prison caseworker, mostly with male inmates. The stories were originally written separately and then later combined with alternating chapters. I started my life as Eileen Clark; married, I became Eileen Stone, and I worked for seven years as Eileen Stone, until the day my divorce was final in 2000. Then I started writing Eileen Clark on all reassessments and Board reports for the next eleven years. Although I was married again, I remained Eileen Clark at work that last month, and then I retired as Eileen Pruett.

At home I had my childhood, my college years, my family, and finally my working years. Working at the prison meant that I dealt with my husband and children in the mornings, evenings, weekends, and holidays. For five days a week, I switched between my home life to my work life and then back again. My two worlds were completely different: home with children; work with convicted criminals. I switched from a loving, caretaking environment to an in-charge rule-oriented, structured situation. One might compare it to changing channels in the mind as I mentally prepared for what I was to deal with as I made the thirty-minute drive to work and home again each day.

At certain points in the reading, the reader may understand how it felt for me to continually switch back and forth during those eighteen and three-fourth years. Then my life changed and things became more integrated for me. The reader also has the choice to read the odd-numbered chapters together and then read the even-numbered chapters together.

Whether it was maturity, life experience, or an eternal plan, I believe it was a good thing for me to bring the parts of my life together so I could feel like one unified person and not two separate and distinct beings.

Chapter ONE

My older sister, Kathleen, would have been six years old when she came home from first grade and took my bottle of milk away from me. After a few swallows, she probably gave it back to me, her four-and-a-half-year-old sibling.

Small-town country life was an easy way to live until... March 13, 1955. Dad, Mom, and their five children climbed in the car as usual on our way to pick up Grandpa Floyd to drive him to work. We stopped in Keene, New Hampshire, to get him and proceeded on the seemingly long drive to the wooden bucket factory where he worked through the week while staying in his one-room "little house." On the way home, Dad decided to stop again to ask Grandma Caroline something.

Grandma Caroline came running out of the house in a panic. "You better get home, your house is burning!" she said. Seven more miles, then we saw it... fully engulfed in flames! Dad told us to stay in the car. We did. Being seven years old, I asked Mom all the questions I could think of while trying to understand what would happen to our family.

The youngest child was fifteen months old when he cried, "I want to go home." I knew we were home, but it was all burning, toys, clothes, house and all. I felt sorry for him, for me, and for all of us. Our house was gone. Fire trucks and many of the townspeople were there, but little could be done. We watched as our house burned down. After a long time, we decided to go and stay with Mom's oldest brother and his family. So that is what we did for the next two weeks until Dad bought a large colonial-style house for $18,000.

Dad believed the fire started by a spark from our wood-burning stove in the front room. That room had a newly varnished floor and wasn't well ventilated due to the cold weather. The fumes could have been the problem. At times, through the years, we would return to our land where the burned out cellar remained and became overgrown with weeds and brush, and pick apples from our trees. I remember Dad entering that house after milking the cow, always with his hat turned around backwards so the visor didn't poke the side of the cow while he milked.

Our next house didn't have a barn, so there was no cow during those years, but Mom got a Rototiller and plowed some land for a garden. There were plenty of rocks to toss out of the way during the first few years of gardening in a new spot. New Hampshire has plenty of rocks, hence the name, "The Granite State" and property lines were made of middle-sized rocks piled along the way. We were free to roam as far as we wanted but were strictly informed never to cross a stone wall, which would have put us outside our eighteen acres. Lots of trees and brush grew; it was fun to wander and explore.

One day, when a brother and I went and looked around, we found what I could only describe as an altar. It was a pile of rocks carefully placed in a round circle about four feet across and maybe four feet tall. The astonishing part was that the top center of the pile must have been used as a pit for fire; those rocks were blackened. My parents didn't know anything about it, whether it had been used for animal sacrifices, cooking or camping or whatever from people long gone. Later I learned that three different Indian tribes had lived there many years before. My other grandfather, Perley, said that some of the wood shingles on the back of his house had been there since the time of Abraham Lincoln, but the Indians would have been around long before that.

Grandpa Perley's house wasn't too many miles into the "woods." His house used to be in town, but there was no town there when we went to visit him. Later I learned that he was in town, but the townspeople moved away into the cities during the depression when they lost their houses. The dirt road to Grandpa's house was never plowed. There were a few months in the winter when he was completely snowed in and alone. When it warmed up, Dad would buy groceries that we would take in to him such as can beans, saltines, Kool-Aid, sugar, lemon drop candies, and other things that Dad knew he liked. Dad took several of us older children and we drove for a while, but then we had to hike that last mile or two through the snow. Plastic grocery bags with handles weren't used then, so we brought our pillowcases and some cloth bags.

Grandpa lived in the large front room, where he had his chair behind a huge loaded oval table. It was covered with empty cans—one had spoon in it—empty saltine boxes, jars, bottles, and just plain stuff he hadn't cleared off. Near Grandpa's chair on the back side of the table was a huge pile of newspapers. I remembered him fingering his way down to a certain spot in the pile and pulling out an empty Kool-Aid package, from where he took a few dollars, handed them to Dad, and asked if he had a few coins to pay the children for helping him carry in the groceries.

Grandpa would ask if it was much trouble carrying the bags through the snow. We just said that we liked to come visit him. Our cousin wrote a book about Grandpa, *Perley: The True Story of a New Hampshire Hermit*. It was fun to read more about him than I knew of. He was a good man, but did go to jail for not paying child support, even though he gave her the house they lived in. We also visited Grandpa in the springtime. He showed us how he would make a hole in a maple tree, then pound a round wood spout into the tree and hang a bucket on the spout. He would go back a few days later and collect what was in the bucket. He let us taste some; it was like sweet water and very good. Then he showed us a shed where the sweet sap got boiled and boiled until it was the thickness of syrup—real maple syrup. He would give Mom a gallon of the syrup, but would sell the rest. Mom said that she was his favorite child.

Mom boiled the maple syrup until it was even thicker. She would tell one of us kids to get some clean snow in a metal pie pan. We had plenty of those since she usually made about thirty pies for Thanksgiving. She tested the thickened syrup to see if it was ready by drizzling a small amount onto the snow. It was either declared ready or we had to wait longer. Then the older kids had to go and get more pie tins of snow so there would be enough for all of us including Dad and her—probably about seven or eight kids at that time. She "served" it by drizzling a stream of the thick syrup over each person's pie plate of snow. We gladly had our forks in hand as we anticipated eating the chewy sweet treat that quickly thickened as soon as she handed each person their pan of snow. It was very good.

Dad decided that we should have something to do while we enjoyed the treat, so it became a tradition that he got out his slide projector and had us set up the screen so we could watch his 35 millimeter slides of the family or of around town. That was always a fun evening to have with the family.

"Sugar on Snow" was what we called it, but we only had it in the early spring, when there was still snow.

The rest of the year, we enjoyed maple syrup on pancakes and French toast. Mom once explained how she could make everyone in the family happy. First she made plenty of the egg and milk mixture and dipped the bread, cooking it for those who wanted French toast. After adding flour and baking powder, she cooked for those wanting plain pancakes. My next younger brother, Warren, and I waited till the end because then she added corn to the pancake mix for those who liked their pancakes with added corn. As Grandpa got older and no longer made maple syrup, Mom bought Mapleine to flavor the sugar and water that she cooked into syrup. It surprised me to learn that you use twice as much sugar as you use of water. Grandpa enjoyed having his goats, usually a few dozen goats, but sometimes there were more when the new little one were born in the spring. He almost always had fresh milk and little goat friends too play with. We never wandered far on Grandpa's land, but he told about how the goats were really good at keeping all of his land cleared of brush and weeds.

What part of his land we did see looked as if a lawn mower and weed eater had been all through and between the trees scattered through his fields.

I liked Grandpa's treadmill. It was outside the front of his house under the roof-covered patio. It was built up high and on quite a slant. Grandpa may have built his treadmill. It was not electric, but he could insert a crank handle to turn it when a goat walked on it. He said the goats needed exercise in the winter months. Then he would let us walk, but he did not crank it. It took us walking with a little pushing motion while we climbed the angle on the treadmill. All too soon, my time was done so my sister and brother could have a turn before Dad wanted to head home. When the snow melted, the whole family would visit Grandpa. I think Mom liked showing him each new baby. Eventually there were ten children. We grew up in rural New Hampshire. It was a good life with most of our cousins living around town. First grade for me and the first two grades for Kathy were spent in the one-room school in the east part of town—the same school that both of my parents attended, with eight grades in a single room.

Grandpa had a lot of goats. Little did I know at that time, we would have goats and that I would one day work in a prison.

Chapter TWO

STEPPING INSIDE THE CAFETERIA, it looked similar to the one at college, except that there were no women, only male inmates who lived and ate in this part of the prison. In fact, I seemed to be the only woman there at that time. I went to lunch that day with my supervisor and a few others. I was warned that the inmates would look, maybe even make a comment or two. A hush fell over the group of inmates, all of them sitting four each around small round tables as we proceeded between them and to the serving line. It was my first day at the prison, not counting the college tour I had taken years before.

I felt them looking, asking questions with their eyes, then whispering comments as I picked up my tray and made my selections. I wore skirt and blouse that day, as one might on their first day of work. The male staff members I was with each straddled the three circular wooden seats that protruded from the round table that was securely fastened to the floor. The last seat was for me. I sat sidesaddle in my skirt, as all watched, and uncomfortably ate my first meal in the prison.

A coworker explained that staff never sits at the same tables with the inmates. Our tables were the ones by the double doors where we entered. To the right of us, were table with four inmates each. They all wore light blue shirts with their prison numbers stamped on the left side of their chest. This didn't seem like prison: no handcuffs, no stripes, and free to walk and mingle, a whole room full of them.

I didn't say much as we ate. Then pretty soon, the inmates all finished eating at the same time. They filed up to the line, removed the plastic cups and plastic utensils, and dumped any remaining food and napkins and walked out. Within minutes, another group filed in, so orderly, as I realized they did this same ritual every day, three times a day, for weeks and months, maybe years for some.

It was such a relief to exit that large room where so many criminals were at all at one time. We proceeded down the hall and out into the sunshine and cool breeze on that memorable spring day. At college, no one cared when I walked into the cafeteria, but here in prison, it was different as I was the spectacle, the one variance in the inmates' daily routine. I was glad that I made it through the whole meal and out the door and nothing had gone wrong. Each day after that was easier.

I learned more each day about what to expect. The cafeteria was only for medium security inmates. If any of them did anything seriously wrong, they would immediately be moved to maximum security housing and fed trays that were delivered to their cells. Another fact learned was that if I ever observed the inmates not eating one particular food item, then it was probably best not to eat it either. Staff supervised inmates who worked in the kitchen preparing the food, but it would still be possible for unknown substances to get into the food. If that happened, word would spread among the inmates not to eat that item that day. I often thought about that possibility, but enjoyed eating the free food that someone else had fixed. In the nine years I ate lunch in that cafeteria, I wasn't aware of any problems with the food. "Homemade" stews were common and bread was made by the inmates during the graveyard shift.

Later, things changed because of gang problems. Security increased and food was therefore delivered to all the housing units in the prison on stacks of trays belted together and loaded onto carts and into trucks. Staff could still eat food from the extra trays delivered to each housing unit for another nine years until budget cuts put a stop to that. Then everyone brought their own food. It was possible to order a meal ahead of time and pay for it, but all that seemed like too much of a bother. I was given a nameplate, a printed copy of the policies and procedures, another smaller notebook of instructions, some blank reassessment forms, and a cardboard box for my "office." My location was the end of a conference room table, where I worked each day. This was convenient to the office next door where I went with any questions.

I learned how to do the housing reassessments. I reviewed the inmates' files and recorded the points of Seriousness of Crime, Length of Incarceration, Criminal Violence History, Escape History, Age, Disciplinary History,

Substance Abuse History, Month Until Release, Seriousness of Current Disciplinaries, Number of Current Disciplinaries, Substance Abuse History in the Last Twelve Months, and Work and Programming Performance. The points determined if an inmate was to drop, remain the same, or advance in custody levels. Too many points meant that the inmate would go to maximum security housing with more hours of lockdown each day. The reassessment documents were then given to more experienced caseworkers who obtained the inmates' signatures.

I was assigned to my own housing unit and dealt directly with the inmates. There were always plenty of "kites" or notes from inmates to answer. Those dealt with all manners of things, since the inmates are always told to ask their caseworker. That first caseload was temporary, three months, while the permanent caseworker went to the Fred House Academy to become POST (Peace Officer Standards & Training) certified, which I also did a short time later.

One of the first things I learned was the difference between a felony and a misdemeanor. There were also different felonies; first degree was more serious than third degree, and all were more serious than misdemeanors. Felons could be put on probation, or the judge could send them to prison. Those committing misdemeanors would only go to jail unless the more serious Class A's chose to serve their year in the prison.

Chapter THREE

I ENJOYED GOING TO school, probably because I did reasonably well and it was at school that I saw my cousins and other friends. The summers seemed long and I would pester my mother, "Mom, what can I do now?" When she suggested work, I would suddenly think of some game to play with my brothers and sisters. One game we played was "Steal the eggs." Since there were six girls and four boys, I often would be on the boys' team against the other girls. First, we would put a few rocks in the grass, marking a line across the center of the lawn. Each team would get eight rocks to put in a "nest" considerably back from the centerline. Then a spot on each side would be designated as the "jail," also back away from the centerline. Each team would be safe on their own side of the line. The object was to run quickly onto the other side to steal a rock (egg) from the other team's nest without being tagged by one of them. If tagged, you went to their jail, until a team member touched and freed you. To win, one team had to get all of the other team's eggs (one at a time) or get all of the other team members in its jail.

    In the winter we might play Monopoly, chess, other table games, or hide-and-seek, or we might have even built tents with blankets and sheets laid over chairs, table, furniture, and clothes pinned together. When we asked Mom if she wanted to play Monopoly with us, she would tell us to get the game set up while she finished washing the dishes. When my second oldest brother, Walter, played, he always tried to get Boardwalk and Park Place. If someone else had one or the other, he would plead and tease and finally buy it from that person. It always amazed the rest of us how many times he would win with just those two pieces. Since we lived in the country, a quarter of a mile or more from any other family with children, we just stayed home and played with our brothers and sisters. One thing I remember was trading toys. We'd make a game of it, usually with four of us. We would each get a toy or something we no longer wanted. Without letting the other see it, we would bring it to one corner of Mom and Dad's bed and hide it under the blanket or sheet. Then we would agree on who would trade with whom, without knowing what you would receive. You had to trade, and if you didn't like what you received, you could just trade it away in the next round. That was how, we—as the older ones—got rid of the toys we no longer wanted. The little kids usually wanted whatever junk we didn't want anymore.

There was a Congregational Church in our small New Hampshire town. It was the only church in town. If you went to church, that was where you went. Usually our family would only go the Sunday before Christmas, Easter, and Mother's Day. It was a matter of sitting for an hour, listening to the choir sing, and the minister preaching his sermon. Then the collection plate was passed. Once every three months the Sacrament was given—perfectly cut squares of white bread with no crusts and grape juice in tiny little glasses. In the summer we attended two weeks of Vacation Bible School, each day Monday through Friday. That was fun. They had crafts and games along with the Bible study, and a graduation and certificate at the end of the two weeks.

I remember that Kathy and I went to PF or Pilgrim Fellowship, which was held every Wednesday evening at the Congregational Church. We read and discussed the New Testament. I liked going because it was for kids, and I was eleven and twelve then. We learned about the life of Jesus and the travels and teachings of the Apostle Paul.

The Congregational Church was where the town's annual Fourth of July bicycle parade was held. Children decorated their bicycles with crepe paper and other things. One year Barbara, a cousin of mine, attached to her bicycle an umbrella with streamers of crepe paper hanging from it. Of course she won first prize. My aunt Helen made fancy decorated cakes. She brought a cake made in the shape of the church. It was on display and looked quite good, but I don't remember eating it. Another time she brought a fancy cake to our house to eat. It was in the shape of a baby carriage with the rounded top to shade the face of the tiny plastic doll that was frosted into it. We did eat that one.

Chapter FOUR

Weekly, we had our caseworker meetings. The supervisor presented her information, then it was her practice to go around the long table and ask each person what they had to say. That's where I first met Laddie. He said he bought something to show us. He lifted a large cardboard box onto the table. He opened it and we beheld a large turtle! He explained how he had found the turtle in Indiana when he and his family had driven home for a vacation. I had never seen one that size. The turtle's shell was as large as a person's hand with its thumb and fingers all stretched out. That seemed to me like a strange thing for a person to bring to a work meeting. After that, Laddie gave us weekly updates of what the turtle was eating and doing. The weekly updates from Laddie about his turtle were welcomed and enjoyed by all. I don't remember how many months afterward it was, but eventually the turtle died.

I found it very helpful to have those weekly meetings in getting to know the other caseworkers. It was a good place to ask questions. Laddie was always there with a lighthearted comment, making an otherwise routine meeting a bit more fun.

After six months learning to do the housing assessments and reassessments, I was assigned to fill in for another caseworker who was going to the Training Academy for three months. That was a regular caseload with about 120 inmates in that housing unit. There weren't as many assessments and reassessments as I had been doing, but I had to learn how to do Board Reports, which included recommendations to the Board of Pardons concerning how much time an inmate should serve in prison, along with a summary of working, programming, and education that he had done while in prison. I hadn't yet dealt with inmates directly, but I had learned a lot about working in a prison, or so I thought.

Up to this point, I only worked twenty hours a week; now it would be full time. A regular caseload meant that, besides paperwork, I would meet with inmates and deal with all sorts of issues. An inmate might need something notarized. At that time, a lady form the records office came daily at a certain time to an area just outside the cafeteria. I would simply instruct inmates to show up there with their paperwork to be notarized. Over time that changed; all caseworkers were told they needed to become notaries. I did. It was part of the job. Later I found out that a few of the caseworkers never did become notaries. They would refer their inmates to other caseworkers.

In those first weeks meeting with inmates, it seemed like they had hundreds of questions, too many to wait until the weekly staff meeting, so I would simply call Laddie or another caseworker and ask their opinion. Not wanting to bother any one person too much, I called different caseworkers. Laddie was always helpful. He gave me copies of various forms I needed. Then I would visit the copy machine regularly to keep a supply on hand. Once, a caseworker whom I called said something I wondered about, so I just called another caseworker with the same question—and received a different answer. At that point, I decided that I could do things my own way and didn't call other caseworkers as often. I had been told not to reveal personal information to inmates, whether I was married, had children, where I lived—things like that. Inmate housing units had several assigned officers there all the time, day and night. As a caseworker, I had an office and could meet with inmates in the office or could talk to them in the housing unit. It was probably the first time when I went down to the housing unit, several inmates gathered around with a variety of questions. After a while, one fellow asked, "So are you married?" Without much hesitation, I answered, "Well, I'm not looking, so I guess it doesn't really matter." I concluded that was a pretty good answer since the other inmates chuckled. I had been polite, given a response without telling him anything personal, and put him in his place. The other inmates found that amusing.

Inmates have plenty of time to work their strategies in very small increments. My first office was in a hallway where inmates needed to pass to get to the infirmary. Some needed to go daily or every few days for regular medications or for diabetic testing. Besides medical reasons, other inmates were in that hallway with a pass and a specific place to go. One fellow who passed by my office regularly, started saying "Hi" each day as he went by.

After a while, he would stand for a few minutes in my doorway, making any kind of conversation he could. Then he started talking longer and longer and stepped just a little further into my office each day. One day as he stopped to talk, he touched my shoulder just lightly, and briefly, as he spoke. That would likely have continued and escalated, but after talking to my supervisor about the situation, I did as she advised and told that inmate that he shouldn't stop and talk anymore, that I had work to do, and that if I needed to see any of the inmates on my caseload, I would let them know. That ended whatever strategy he might have been planning.

Inmates were always happy to tell me how things worked in the prison, but I learned that it was wise to verify what the inmates told me. One inmate explained that they had a barber person on staff who cut the inmates' hair; but there were just too many inmates, so he had an unofficial pair of scissors and he would cut hair for a candy bar or some other commissary item. He told me that the officers knew he cut hair and let him do so. The officers' Captain or Lieutenant might walk down the housing unit, doing there inspections, and tell the officers which inmates needed haircuts. Rather than complain about not having enough barbers, they just let that inmate, and maybe others, do the hair cutting. Later, I learned that inmates cutting other inmates' hair might happen in the main population in the prison, but would never be allowed in maximum security housing. In maximum security, there was a very strict list of items that inmates were allowed to have; scissors was definitely not among the allowed items. Scissors may not have been allowed in main population, either, but at least that one inmate had a pair.

Thinking about scissors reminds me of the time that my office in medium security was to be painted. I came to work one day and found my desk and everything from my office out in the main corridor where unescorted inmates had to pass by to get to the infirmary. When I had moved into that office, some supplies had been left by the previous caseworker. Among them was a pair of scissors with a blade at least six inches long. Seeing my desk unattended in the hallway, I immediately checked the top drawer and breathed a sigh of relief as I saw the long-bladed scissors were still there. Anyone going by could have gone through the desk, but it didn't seem as though anyone had. The scissors—as was everything else—were still there. I found out that my office had been painted over the weekend.

The actual painting crew was made up of inmates with a staff member supervising, but I still felt a bit exposed with all my things not locked up and just out there in the hallway. The next day, everything was back to normal and my office was locked when I wasn't there.

There was one time in my early days of working in the prison that I had occasion to be working in an older part of the building that had older cells and old locking mechanisms that had a particularly large key—maybe six or eight inches long. I was having a lot of trouble and just couldn't make that key work. I knew it was the right one but just couldn't do it. A very helpful inmate noticed my difficulty and offered to help. I didn't realize any other staff were nearby or I would have asked them for help. Instead, I gave the small key ring with the large key to the inmate who attempted to make the key work. An officer came by, saying, "I'll take that" as he took the key from the inmate and seemed to know how to make it work. I sure heard about that one later. We were *Not* supposed to give keys to inmates. Later I learned that it was a real big deal when any key was lost. Every effort was made to find it, including cell searches and inmate interviews. A report was then written, and there would be consequences.

During those first few years, I worked only in medium security housing, sometimes called main population. Whenever there were threats, fights, or other problems among inmates, any one of them could, and would, be moved to maximum security and, thereafter, locked in his cell most of the day. As a result, most inmates behaved most of the time.

But they were still inmates, and all had been convicted of crimes, some even violent crimes.

Chapter FIVE

IT WAS IN 1962 when the LDS (Church of Jesus Christ of Latter-day Saints) missionaries first came to our house. One other LDS family was in our small town of three hundred or so. Mom and Dad always suspected that they suggested that the missionaries to come to our house. Dad said they looked like insurance salesmen dressed in their suits. They came back each week and taught us the lessons. The missionaries asked if we had a Bible. Dad told me where it was and to go get it. When I brought it back and handed it to him, it was covered with thick dust. Later, Dad said that I should have brushed it off before bringing it out. I guess it was pretty obvious that it hadn't been read recently. The missionaries came once a week and I looked forward to it. One week, Mom invited her aunt to come over when missionaries were coming. The aunt came along with her minister. They talked quite a while, and afterwards Dad commented how well the missionaries did for being so young.

Each week, after the missionaries' lessons, we would talk with them more and more, and finally at 10:30 p.m., they would say that they had to leave, that the Spirit goes to bed at 10:30. Then we would sit around talking about things they said, and our observation about how they had notes and things behind the flannel board they were using. I just knew that they couldn't have that much stuff memorized.

Around that time Kathy, Warren, and I went to 4-H Camp for a week. Warren had been wrestling other boys on the army-type cots that they slept in, when he fell and cut his head just above his eye on the corner of the wrought iron bed frame. As a result, he needed stitches.

The time came to be baptized in the LDS Church. It was the wrong time of the month for Mom, so she said she would just wait until my brother had his stitches out. Dad, my next younger sister, Priscilla, my next brother,

Walter, and I were baptized on July 26, 1962, at the Joseph Smith Memorial in Sharon/South Royalton, Vermont, by the missionaries. Mom and Warren were baptized a few weeks later, and Kathy was baptized six months later. Kathy told me that she believed almost everything except for the part about Joseph Smith being a prophet and didn't want to be baptized until she knew for sure. Near the Joseph Smith Memorial is the hearthstone of where the original house was that Joseph Smith's family lived in when he was born in 1805. I remember the wonderfully clean and pure feeling I carried with me as we traveled through the countryside and toward home the day that I was baptized.

Then we became involved in the youth activities of the Church. I remember softball games, youth conferences, speech competitions, and weekly MIA (Mutual Improvement Association) meetings on Tuesday nights. I looked forward to MIA because I only saw my Church friends on Sundays and Tuesdays.

It was at one of these softball games when I was playing the catcher position that I caught a bat in the face. As I was standing behind the batter waiting to catch the ball, the batter swung and hit it pretty well. Then he let the bat swing around behind him and released it while running for first base. Blood was bleeding from my mouth. My two front lower teeth were loose. I was taken to a doctor or dentist (or someone), and they said that my teeth should be okay and that I probably wouldn't lose them—I didn't. I don't remember playing the position of catcher any more after that.

I went to the first grade in a one-room school that taught eight grades. There was no running water. There was a jug with a spout to turn to get a drink. The bathroom was an attached outhouse on the back of the building. Most buildings in our small New Hampshire town were quite old. Most grades must have only had three or four students each since there were about thirty students total for all the eighth grades. There was electricity, but I also remember a wood stove for heat. I only went to first grade at the old one-room school in the east part of town, 1953 to 1954. It is now a home, since the new elementary school was built in the center of town in 1954. In this new school, there were two classrooms, each with four grades. Mrs. Harris was my grammar school teacher and had been the teacher in the old school. She was strict with discipline. She would use a twelve-inch ruler over the back of a student's hand or throw a chalkboard eraser to get a student's attention.

Occasionally, she raised her voice at students, but I remember always being good and doing fairly well, so I earned praise and liked that. For reading, one grade of students was called to sit around a long wooden table at the front of the room. We took turns reading, as the others were expected to follow along watching the words. Flash cards for the math tables were fun. One grade would stand in a row with Mrs. Harris holding the cards. When she showed the card, whoever guessed the answer got the card. Addition, subtraction, multiplication, and then division were learned that way. The one with the most cards won. My favorite card was $7 \times 8 = 56$. I almost always got that card. The new school had one room for first to fourth grades with Mrs. Harris, and the other room for fifth to eighth grades with Mrs. Wilbur.

When I was in sixth grade, we got a new teacher, Mr. Whitham. The only LDS Church members in our town were from his family. I liked having a man for a teacher. When we got to know him better at Church, sometimes he would ask me to babysit for his children so he and his wife could go out. At school, we played tag, hopscotch, marble games, and Red Rover, Red Rover.

At supper time, I would set the table, usually at my mother's first request—then I wouldn't have to help wash or dry the dishes—or I would clear the table and stack the dishes, then say, "Mom, would you like me to get someone else to dry the dishes for you?" Mom usually washed the dishes by hand and could keep up with three of us drying and putting them away.

Another thing I learned from Mom was to immediately hang up my coat when I took it off because Mom would look around and see whose stuff (of the older kids) was laying around. That person had to pick up twice as many items or toys as compared to how many items of their own stuff was laying around.

Chapter SIX

ON MY FIRST PERMANENT caseload, I met an inmate I shall call Bill for purposes of this story and for confidentiality reasons. Bill's name was on my list of Board reports to do for that month. I went to bring the Board application to him. The officers told me that Bill lived on the second level. The officers' station was located on the first level and usually two or three officers were on duty in the station. When it came time to count the inmates they would go upstairs and walk up and down the halls with cells on both sides. When I went up the stairs and down the hallway, most of the inmates were milling around or in their cells, all with the doors slid open. As I approached Bill's cell to give him the application that I needed him to complete, I noticed he was in his cell, so I stepped in the doorway to his cell and held out the paperwork. After verifying who he was, I explained that I needed to do his Board report, and so I handed him the application and asked him to fill it out.

He was very polite, easy to talk to, with no apparent tattoos and not at all scary looking. I again explained that I needed for him to fill out the application so I could do his Board report prior to his Board hearing. He took the paperwork, listening to everything I said, and then started explaining some things about his case and how he was convicted. The things he said were interesting.

He continued talking, and then as he himself backed up, said, "Why don't you just step forward one or two steps and not be in the doorway?" He spoke so matter-of-factly that as he moved himself back, I did take the two steps as he suggested. He continued talking about his case and things that weren't right about it. Then I heard a noise and noticed that the cell door was sliding shut, along with all the other inmates' cell doors. I could see that I wouldn't make it through the closing cell door, so I didn't try. Bill reassured me, saying that it was okay, that the officers would be along for count and that it would only be five or ten minutes before the cell doors would all open. I sure felt stupid at that moment, and even more ridiculous as the officer doing count came along and noticed that I, a caseworker, was locked in the cell with an inmate.

Thinking back on that incident, I realize that the inmate knew exactly what time count was, and exactly what would happen. I am sure that he enjoyed my dilemma, as did several other inmates nearby who could see what had happened. I found Bill and most inmates enjoyable to work with, but I was, at that time, quite unfamiliar with the routine of life as an inmate. After admitting how stupid I felt-probably more than once to Bill finally the cell doors opened, and I moved out into the hallway as we talked a bit longer. You can be sure that from that point on, I inquired about the count times and when the inmates had to be in their cells. Very few times after that did I ever step inside an inmate's cell again.

Bill explained that he didn't want to see the Board of Pardons, that he was still working on his appeal. He said that he did not commit the crimes that he was in prison for. Bill continued telling me more about his case. I wondered if it was possible that an innocent man could be in prison. Then he pulled a notebook down from a shelf and said there was something he wanted to show me.

Over the next few months, I read Bill's prison file, including the police reports, and had more conversations with him about his case. Many things pointed to the fact that Bill could be telling the truth, but the jury had convicted him. I realized that it was possible for someone to "con" me, but I figured it would be hard for Bill to "con" the other inmates, so I took an informal survey as I talked to other inmates. Individually, I asked if they believed it was possible that some inmates could Be "Not Guilty" of the crimes they were in prison for—and I asked, of the inmates in our unit, who would they say might not be guilty. Each inmate gave several names, and Bill's name was the only one on every list. So, other inmates who knew Bill also believed him.

Bill had taken a lie detector test. It was in his file. It showed he was telling the truth, so he was given another one. The second lie detector test also showed he was being honest, so he was given a third one; the results of that one were shown to be inconclusive!

Chapter SEVEN

I REMEMBER FUN TIMES when the electricity would go out. Dad and Mom had a kerosene lantern that had a glass chimney that covered a wick that could be adjusted. The bottom of the wick extended down into the kerosene, a clear liquid, of which filled the bottom of the lantern. Only Mom or Dad used the matches to light the lantern. Then we would sit around the large dining room table and play games. Board games were possible if you were near enough to the lantern.

Sometimes we played ghost, where one person would say a letter to start the game. Then each person adds a letter to the word, but tries not to finish any word. If you did, then you became one-third ghost, then two-thirds, and then at three-thirds, you were eliminated from playing. If someone challenged you, and you didn't have a possible word in mind including the letter you just said, you also earned one-third ghost. Sometimes it seemed too bad when the lights and electricity came back on after a few minutes, or a few hours, or whatever it was, because everyone quit playing together and went back to whatever they might have been doing in their room or elsewhere.

After always taking lunch to school, I felt almost grown up when the new high school was built and in ninth grade bought school lunch. It was 35 cents per day. I turned sixteen in eleventh grade, and then got my first job that spring. I worked at Cheshire County Savings Bank in their mortgage department. After the loan officers finished the paperwork, setting up a new mortgage, we organized the paperwork and made up the mortgage payment books and sent them out.

I did make the girls' varsity basketball team in school and I still have the certificate showing I earned a letter "M" for our high school. The rules of basketball have changed since then. We had six on the team, with three Forwards and three Guards. One of each position got to be "roving" and would play on the entire court, so there were two Forwards and two Guards that were restricted to their own half of the court. I played as a Guard. The best part was that we always got milk and cookies after the games. I was also in National Honor Society (for having good grades) and in the chess club.

I didn't wear makeup in high school. As far as boys were concerned, I probably had half a dozen secret crushes until I was a senior. Then I actually dated a few times.

I didn't have the money for a dress to wear to prom, and I didn't like asking my parents because we had a big family, so I bought the fabric and decided to sew a dress. I was very proud of it, so I saved a piece of each of the two kinds of fabric. My experience with sewing started a few years prior. First I made an apron in 4-H Club. That was easy enough. Then I borrowed one of Mom's patterns for a bathrobe. Since I was a little smaller than she was, I cut down the size of the pattern—one inch from the edge of all pieces. That didn't work quite as well as I thought. The sleeves were snug and almost too tight, while the robe was still quite long. After that, I either sewed doll clothes or bought patterns at the size that I needed. Mom also taught me to crochet and eventually to knit, skills that came in handy later during the times at home raising children.

From the day I joined the Church at thirteen years old, I looked forward to and dreamed of the day that I would go to Brigham Young University, BYU, in Utah. Actually, there was a specific reason I looked forward to going to BYU: there was a guy I met at the wedding reception of a girl in our Keene, New Hampshire Branch of the LDS Church. She married a return missionary. They were having a reception and the return missionary's whole family came. The brother of the returned missionary was only a year older than I was then, in the spring of my senior year. He was tall and good-looking in his suit, although he did look young for his age. We spent several hours talking that day. Then he gave me his address, so we wrote letters that summer until I went to BYU where he was. We dated my freshman year, and then he went on his two-year mission for the Church. I sort of figured that we might get married when he got back.

Meanwhile, there were two other guys that I might mention. One was a building missionary and was allowed to dance with girls, unlike the proselyting missionaries. On building missions, the missionaries were assigned to areas that were building chapels, as our LDS group, the Keene

Branch was. A few LDS members meeting together weekly are a branch. Six or eight branches meet together twice a year and that group is called a district. Over the years as membership in the branches increase, they become wards. Then those wards meet twice a year as a stake. At that time, our Keene Branch met in an old G.A.R. Hall (Grand Army of the Republic). At Christmastime, our branch held a dance. The building missionary was there. He was playing Santa Claus and was dressed accordingly. We danced a few times. I guess he liked me more than I realized at the time. Towards the end of the dance, he asked if I would go downstairs with him because he wanted to talk to me. We talked for a while, and he said he really liked me and would I consider—sometime in the future—if maybe we got married. I talked about the fact that I had just barely turned fifteen and that I didn't know what the future would bring, but I would think about it. The he was transferred to another area. I didn't think too much more about that conversation at that time.

Members were encouraged to volunteer their time assisting the building missionaries working on the chapel, so I did when school was out for the summer. Dad would drop me off on his way to work and pick me up afterwards. I helped with whatever construction they were working on at the time. I remember the tedious work of smoothing the soft concrete between the concrete blocks using the metal grouting tool. It was shaped like a stretched out letter S made of a metal straw cut in half the long way and bent with a curve in the middle. Dad said that I probably put in more volunteer hours that summer than anyone else in the branch. Another building missionary was there, so it was fun volunteering. I really liked that fellow, and he came back when his mission was over, but I was planning to go to BYU in Utah. Then he dated another girl in the ward and married her.

Meanwhile, during that summer before going to BYU, I wrote letters to both the younger brother of the returned missionary who married my girlfriend and to the first building missionary who had played Santa at the dance. When I got to BYU, that building missionary was at home and lived seventy miles north of BYU, so he only drove down to see me a couple of times. One of those times he visited was when I invited him to an open house in our dormitory. One Sunday afternoon a month, our girls' dorm was "opened" for a couple of hours for guys to visit in our rooms (with the doors open). My roommate was there, too. She had not invited anyone. So the three of us, two girls and a guy, were talking when the future missionary I was dating showed up. He had found out about the open house and came over to see me. For a little while, it worked out okay. I think both guys thought that the other one was there my roommate. But then she fell asleep and it became clear that both were my friends. As we talked, I think they both must have felt as uncomfortable as I did. I had written letters to both of them throughout the summer, but I had only invited one to the open house. Finally, the time expired and both had to leave.

The former building missionary invited me to his family's house for the Thanksgiving holiday weekend. I met his younger sister. As I talked with her, she said something about her brother and me getting married . . . whoa . . . I didn't realize that we were officially engaged. So, before I left his home that weekend, I broke it off. That was the end between him and me, but it was okay; I liked the future proselyting missionary better. He was only one year older that I was, unlike the other fellow who was four or five years older.

Chapter EIGHT

Smoking had been allowed for inmates, but that changed. Inmates were no longer allowed to buy cigarettes on commissary. They were given a few weeks to finish smoking the cigarettes they already had purchased. At the time of the cutoff, Laddie and I were assigned to give a Smoking Cessation class. After some instruction, we gave the inmates previously prepared baggies of snacks with carrot and celery sticks and other veggies. One sandwich bag each was likely not nearly enough to help addicted smokers make it through an entire week until the next class and the next baggie of snacks. One fellow I remember, who had smoked for twenty or thirty years, seemed okay at the first class, but then seemed like he had a cold after one week without a cigarette. Two weeks later, he appeared completely wiped out, with cold and flu symptoms and just sitting there miserably, not talking or even interacting with the discussion. Just existing seemed to be all he could manage after going cold turkey two weeks prior. He improved and gradually seemed to get better in the weeks that followed. I enjoyed giving that class with Laddie, who was quite comfortable dealing with the male inmates.

Then came the other time I stepped inside an inmate's cell. I knew it wasn't count time. I was walking in the housing unit when an inmate asked about a particular form. I had come prepared and had the paper he wanted. I explained that I needed to watch him sign it, but that I didn't have a pen on me. He proceeded into his cell to get a pen. Needing to watch him sign, I followed him. On the edge of his desk area (it was really just a shelf protruding outward) lay a lit cigarette, carefully placed with the lit end hanging off the edge. Apparently, he had laid it down when he saw me and came out to ask about the form he needed. Then, without thinking, he led me back into his cell. There the cigarette was, an obvious rule violation, since cigarettes were no longer allowed. I acted as if I didn't see it. Later, however, I knew what I had to do. I had to write the incident report and the disciplinary for the violation. Whoever saw the incident first was the one who was responsible to write the report. Others could write additional information if it was warranted. Usually my role as a caseworker meant that I did things, within policy, to help inmates, but not this time. The inmate knew I had seen the cigarette, and he had to know that I followed the rules, so I prepared the incident report and the disciplinary.

At that time, inmates in medium security housing wore light blue button-up shirts, with each inmate's numbers stamped on the chest pocket of the shirt. Most of the inmates wore obviously ironed shirts: creases were ironed in all manner of directions. Inmates would buy their weekly allotment of commissary, and then a package of cupcakes (or another item) would be "paid" to the inmate who did their ironing for them. A lot of inmates might earn 40 cents an hour for four hours a day, but some jobs paid as much as $1.25 per hour for forty hours per week. Those jobs were usually for the Correctional Industries and might be in the sign shop, the furniture shop, data entry, the license plate plant, or in the print shop. There was also a greenhouse and a sewing shop.

I enjoyed the greenhouse. I could go there and choose a beautiful flowering plant for my office. The only rule was to bring the plant back if it started to look sick. I never killed any of the plants, but I would exchange a plant when it no longer had flowers on it. I remember one plant had a huge ball of flowers, probably at least two feet across. I received all the compliments for the flowers but didn't have to do the work, just a little water and exchange it periodically before it died.

One day an inmate I was meeting with commented on my office chair. He worked in the furniture shop and said how he could easily get my chair recovered with scraps of material that they had. I let him take it on a Friday afternoon and was very pleased with the results the next week. I suppose going through proper channels would have meant filling out paperwork and getting a requisition, and it may only have been possible to have a new chair bought by the state. I thought it was great, getting it done for free, and receiving some donated inmate labor.

Other inmate creations that I benefited from—or should I say my state-owned office benefited from—were hand-drawn pictures and some little handmade rose sculptures. The pictures were simply done with colored pencils and art paper that inmates could purchase on commissary. The roses were the interesting items. The inmate claimed, and it was probably true, that he took bread, cut off the crust, and squeezed and shaped it after mixing in ground-up colored pencil lead. Small pink petals were on a green stem displayed in a small pink vase.

Another inmate saw it, and created a similar rose, but his was displayed in a homemade open-faced box filled with cotton, all made from commissary or scrounged items. Favorite items to use for various projects might be the layer of foil from the package of chips bought on commissary or corn dog sticks collected from a lot of inmates after a corn dog meal.

I was particularly impressed by the inmate who would hand-bind books. He showed me one that he said he had rebound with plenty of thread or string. There is a good chance his string had come from a sheet. Making greeting cards was something that a lot of inmates would do; then they would have something to mail out to their wife, girlfriend, or child.

One inmate told me that he couldn't afford to pay child support while he was in prison, so he just sent small amounts of money directly to his children—then they would know he hadn't forgotten about them. Inmates didn't actually have possession of any coins or cash. The Inmate Accounting Office had a system of their own cheeks that were sequentially numbered. When requested, the housing officer would give the inmate one check to fill out including the name and address it was to be mailed to; the officer then collected it and put it in a particular manila envelope that was taken daily to Inmate Accounting. Inmate Accounting then issued a Bank Check or Money Order and mailed it.

Chapter NINE

THINGS SETTLED DOWN FOR a while since I was only seeing one guy. Most of the time I saw him was over at the house his parents owned, where he lived with his brother and brother's wife (who was my girlfriend from New Hampshire). He was saving money for his mission, so we didn't spend much on dates. We talked a lot, and I think it was understood that we would get married when he returned from his mission. He went to Arizona as a missionary to the Navajo people. He wrote letters to me from his mission, and in every letter, he wrote several paragraphs about the Navajo people and their customs and various people they were teaching. That part of the letter was separate from other general stuff he wrote. Those special parts . . . I copied over and was saving for him in a sort of missionary journal. That was how he was sharing his mission with me.

Then I said good-bye to my roommate and the other girls in the dorm, and went back to New Hampshire that summer after my freshman year at BYU. Then I said good-bye again to my family and returned once again to BYU for my second year of college. I had a new roommate, but missed my missionary who was fulfilling his commitment. My roommate told me that I didn't need to sit home on Friday and Saturday nights just because I was writing to a missionary.

It was February of 1968 when I met Don. He walked up and introduced himself to me. Our first date was a movie. Don asked what I would like to see. I didn't know much about any movies that were currently playing, except for *The Graduate*. I had read about it in responses written to the editorial column in the *Daily Universe*, BYU's campus newspaper. Everything I read said how good it was. I didn't realize till later that it was R-rated. We were watching the movie and Don offered to get some popcorn. He returned during an R-rated scene, sat down, and neither of us said a word. Later, he admitted that he was surprised and wouldn't have taken me to that movie if he had known what the scenes were like. I felt bad for him as he apologized about the movie; after all, he had asked me what I wanted to see.

Don and I dated from February to May of 1968. One special date I remember was to a formal dance that he asked me to attend. He called my roommate and asked her what color the dress was that I would be wearing. Then Don brought me a corsage with the flower petals dipped or dyed in the same color, a bluish green.

As we got to know each other, Don told me about a real challenge that he faced while growing up. His eyesight was really bad and his parents didn't realize it. He would do chores, trying to please his parents, but would be punished for how poorly he did his work. I felt sorry for him as he told me those things.

Don always seemed to have enough money to take me to movies, dances, or wherever we happened to go. He and I got along pretty well, and the missionary was gone.

Sometimes Don said negative things about himself, and I would point out how I saw things about him being an intelligent person and that he always was nice to me. One day, Don was putting himself down and said something to the effect, "Who would ever marry me?"

I said, "I don't know. Have you ever asked anyone? You have never asked me."

Then as Don continued looking down at the street, he said, "Well, would ya?"

"Would I what?"

"Would you marry me?"

Suddenly I felt like I had boxed myself into a corner. I liked the missionary, but he wasn't here. I didn't want to hurt Don, so I said "Yes"—almost in a quizzical tone, as if I was not sure if I meant it.

Later, things seemed okay. I had said I would marry Don, so I figured I should stick with the plan. I went to my "Dorm Mother" with the engagement ring, and my candle-passing was arranged. That night, the ring was placed on a candle. The candle was lit and passed around the circle of girls in my dorm, as we all sang love songs. When the candle came to me, I blew it out; thus announcing my engagement to all the girls in my dorm. They were all happy for me. I felt sad as I thought about the missionary, who had been gone a year by that time.

My plan was that we would wait a year from then to get married. I very much wanted to be sure that I would graduate from college. By waiting a year to get married, I would only have one year of school left. Don agreed. However, after everyone knew of the engagement, he said that he wanted to be married that September, and that there were other "fish" in the sea—that if I didn't want to marry him, he would marry someone else, but he was going to get married that fall. I remember thinking that I had already said that I would marry him, so, if it was to be him, I guess I just needed to go along with what he wanted.

Soon after being engaged, it was time for me to go home to New Hampshire for the summer. Don stayed at BYU and worked full time and went to school full time. We wrote letters during the summer until we were married in September. On September 7, I flew back to Provo and stayed in his apartment while he stayed at the Bishop's house until we were married. The missionary's sister in-law was my friend and wanted to come with us when we got married. Don didn't allow it since he didn't have anyone going with him. I never told her exactly when we were to be married, so it was just the two of us. Don came by the apartment, picked me up, and we drove to Manti. His parents were not members of the Church and so couldn't come to the temple with us. My parents lived in New Hampshire and couldn't afford to make the trip to Utah. We went to the Manti temple by ourselves and were married. Then we drove back to the apartment in Provo. After three or four days, we took a weekend trip, driving to Denver, where his parents had a reception dinner at a local restaurant with seventeen people. Afterward, several of them came back to his parents' house where they had gifts for us.

We continued college until we graduated in August 1971. It was just two of us for four and a half years. I had grown up with nine brothers and sisters, so married life with just my husband and me was quiet. We got along pretty well and I learned to care deeply for him. I remember he preferred going to bed and getting up early to do his homework. My choice would have been to stay up late to finish my homework, and then go to bed; but it worked better for us doing it the same way, so we did it his way.

Graduation day finally came. I made it; I graduated from college, but I gave up my plan to become a high school math teacher. Rather than taking a comprehensive math test, I switched math to my minor and then majored in child development and family relations. Part of the reason for that was because when we were managing a motel, I realized I wouldn't be able to student teach since one of us always had to be at the motel.

Chapter TEN

ONCE THERE WAS AN accident. I think about nine inmates were to be transported from our facility to another prison. That was usually routine, except this time it was winter, and the van had an accident. I don't know the details of the accident, but when we heard about it in the prison, a few caseworkers were called to immediately go through those inmates' files to call family members and inform them of the accident before they heard about it on the news. At that point, we had no information as to the seriousness of the accident, or even which inmates were hurt seriously or if some were dead. I was responsible to call three families. I called them and explained there had been an accident, but could not say how badly their child, father, or brother had been hurt. Desperately they asked questions, but I didn't know any details to tell them. I did mention the hospital that they had been taken to, and I gave them the phone number that I was given so they could call back later to ask for any updates or details as they became available. The families were quite frustrated, and so called back the phone number I had given them. As it turned out, it was the same phone number in the room that we were calling from. I felt rather ridiculous speaking to those same folks again, with no more information to tell them.

Another time I was home from work sleeping when I got a phone call from the prison in the middle of the night. An inmate on my caseload had died. I was told that I needed to come in to work as soon as possible. When I arrived, I was told what had happened. The inmate was diabetic. Prison investigators were there and had questioned the inmate's cellmate, other nearby inmates, and staff. I was told that I would be going with one of the investigators to the inmate's parents' house to inform them of his passing. Nothing seemed real, going to work in the middle of the night and having to do something so out of the ordinary.

The investigator drove; neither of us said much. He pulled into the driveway of the address we had. Then he pulled out his phone and called someone. I thought that was rather strange. Here we were with an important errand to perform, and he was calling someone, his wife, who? I wondered why we didn't just walk up and knock on the door. That was in the days before cell phones were very common. When he spoke, then I understood. He explained to the person on the other end of the phone that we were from the prison and that we were sitting in his driveway, and asked if we could come in because we needed to talk to him. Before long, the door opened and we were admitted to a small well-kept living room. The house was occupied by just one older gentleman whose wife had died. We told him as much as we knew about how his son died. He just listened, and quietly asked a few questions. After our condolences, we left. It had seemed so much nicer to be able to tell him about his son in person, rather than on the phone with few details.

More common than those experiences were the times I received a phone call from an inmate's family member explaining that someone in the family has died and could they speak to the inmate. I would ask for the hospital or mortuary so I could verify their information, and then we agreed on a time for them to call back when I would have the inmate in my office so they could speak about the family member that died. Most of the time, it was legitimate and the phone call was provided to the inmate. Often the inmate showed emotion and even cried a bit. After the phone call, I talked to the inmate for a while as he regained his composure. No inmate wanted to return to his cell and let his cellmate or others see him crying. However, there have been a few instances where inmates appeared to care, yet spent only five minutes discussing the late family member, and then immediately turned the conversation to what that person could do for them. Could they send him some money? Could they sell his car or truck? Could they check his apartment and get his stuff moved out and into storage? I thought it was sad, how those guys felt that others ought to do things for them because they were in prison and couldn't do those things for themselves.

I suppose one experience I will remember for a long time was about an inmate who hanged himself He had committed a serious sex offense against a young child and had been in prison for fifteen years. Finally, he was paroled. After he had been out of prison for a few months, he committed another sex crime and was sent back to prison. He knew that he would be in prison for a long time and apparently couldn't handle the thought of so many years inside again after having had a taste of freedom for those few months. He therefore committed suicide. He was found hanging by the neck with a bedsheet tied around his neck, tight enough that he was slightly higher than what would have been a sitting position on the floor right next to the bars, his legs extended in front of him. He could easily have stood up if he had wanted to.

After a serious incident like suicide, it was the practice to have a debriefing for any staff members involved to discuss the incident and see if anything could or should be done differently in the future. My job as a caseworker was to go through the inmate's file and history, and write and present an overview at the debriefing of him and his life. It truly was sad to see what his past had been like. He had been an ongoing sexual victim as a child, had lost a parent, had to deal with an unloving stepparent, and had been victimized in school and in the military. Given his life history, it is not surprising that he became a perpetrator. It is easy to think that years of therapy should have helped this man, but it is hard to know what being a victim so many times does to a person.

Chapter ELEVEN

The opportunity to manage the Uptown motel in Provo came six months after we were married. The problem was that one of us had to be there all the time, so I dropped out of day school and took evening classes and home-study courses. My goal was to graduate, which I did, but I knew that Don's education was important for the benefit of our future family. We received special permission for my diploma to be moved to where his was to be handed out on graduation day, since only his parents were coming from Denver. New Hampshire was too far for my parents to come.

The motel is no longer there on 469 West Center Street in Provo. There were about thirty rooms for us to rent out. We had a large two-room apartment in back of the motel office.

It was nice to have the use of the swimming pool but, like going to the grocery store, we had to do everything so that one person was always available to rent out rooms. That even applied to Church, with one going in the morning for Sunday School and the other going in the evening for Sacrament meeting. Every day or two, Don would make a bank deposit of the money taken in. For motel supplies, we just let the owner know what was needed and he brought them. We were paid as managers, but sometimes if needed, I punched in on a time card and cleaned a few rooms. Usually there were two maids through the winter and a third in the summer.

Once a man walked in to rent a room. Usually the renters would write down their license number, but this fellow didn't have a car. As he talked, he explained that he didn't have much at all. He was in constant pain from some medical problem, his wife had left him, and had other problems. He seemed to want to talk, but Don didn't since it was very late. The next morning, I checked in to clean some of the rooms. His room was on my list. Without a car, we didn't know whether or not he was still in his room, so Don knocked, and with no answer unlocked the room and went in. The man was found hanging from his closet bar with his belt around his neck. We called the police and they took care of the rest.

Usually renting rooms was uneventful. The person listed their address as they checked in. If someone left something in their room, it was a simple matter to mail it to them. Once I did that and received a response that it was probably not worth the postage for me to return a T-shirt to them. Another time, a maid found a small case with separate sections. In each section were six or eight or more tiny stones that looked like diamonds. That motel client and salesman was really happy to get that little case back. Then there was the time that a guy checked in and mentioned that he needed a couple of extra towels. I wasn't busy and the motel maids had already gone home, so I went to the laundry room and got the towels. I then knocked on the door of the room I had rented to that fellow. He opened the door, took the towels from me and said, "I'm not going to invite you in." Thinking that was odd. I mentioned it to my husband, who said that I had offered him a personal service and maybe he thought I expected something for it. I was never sure whether he was refusing me a tip or something else that I didn't want. After managing that motel for two years, we managed another motel for three months.

Then we bought a single-wide mobile home. Don built the patio and covering. When we lived there, there was one significant incident I remember. I was working at a drapery shop, and Don worked for Provo City. One day we happened to come home for lunch; we didn't always. Just as we drove up to our place, we saw flames flare up in our neighbor's mobile home. Don immediately went over. The door was locked, so he banged on the door. Two small children opened the door. They were home alone. The curtain above the gas stove caught on fire on the trash piled next to the stove just as we happened to arrive there. We called the police and were so thankful to be able to save the lives of those two children. About a year later, we bought a double-wide modular home in Leisure Village in Provo, Utah.

We wanted to start a family, but that didn't seem to happen at first. We eventually started looking into adoption, but that ended up not being necessary because our first child came along four and a half years after we were married. Susan was such a joy.

I thought I knew what to do with a baby. I had been the second of my parents' ten children and felt like I had some experience with the younger ones. Sometimes situations arose when I wasn't quite sure what to do. Don would talk to his middle-aged secretary at work, then come home and say, "Sally said you should do this or that." I did not want to hear what "Sally said." My daughter was my baby. I had worked full time at the drapery shop; now I was a full time mother. Fifteen months later we had our son, Brady. That was easier since Susan had Brady to play with, which entertained both of them.

Chapter TWELVE

OVER THE YEARS, SECURITY throughout the prison has increased whenever incidents happened. When I worked in maximum security housing, I remember doing groups with other caseworkers. I suppose it was more dangerous than I realized, but I was fortunate and nothing serious happened to me. My caseload consisted of half of that housing unit. The other caseworker was a fellow. We posted a paper letting the inmates know that we would be conducting an anger management group. Quite a few inmates sent notes expressing their interest in attending the group. From that group, we selected the participants, eight or ten I think.

The inmates in that unit were in their cells, each with a cellmate, for twenty-three hours a day. They had one hour a day to go into the larger open area in front of all the cells in that section. They could use the telephone, shower, or simply run around in that larger space. With those limits, it is clear why many inmates would be interested in attending a group or class to be out of their cells.

We had one radio between us and could contact the housing officers if needed. The officers brought the inmates we requested from their cells to the classroom we were using. We, about ten of us, each sat on plastic stools around the edges of that room. We went around the room, with each inmate talking about himself and what he wanted or expected to get out of the group. That session went fine and all inmates were returned to their cells with no problems. After that first session, other inmates became aware of which inmates were called out for the group. Therefore, we were contacted by another inmate saying how much he wanted to be in the group. We allowed him to join, but shouldn't have as we later found out.

That next time in group, we had the officers bring out the same inmates along with the new fellow. That new inmate asked to use the bathroom, which we let him do since there was a bathroom just a couple doors down the hall. He came back and the group proceeded for about half an hour. The same inmate again requested to use the bathroom, saying that he had diarrhea and really needed to go. We again let him, not thinking too much about it. That group session ended, we radioed the officers that we were finished, and then escorted the inmates halfway down the hall until the officers came to finish taking them back to their cells.

Later, the other caseworker and I found out what happened next. Just prior to the inmates separating to go half each into different sections, there was a scuffle. One inmate had grabbed the back of the neck of another inmate. The two officers immediately separated them, but blood was coming from one guy's neck. Reinforcements and medical were called and the situation was taken care of. Later, the other caseworker and I heard about how the newest inmate to the group, had a homemade knife or shank taped on him where it hadn't been obvious, but could easily be used when he chose to. We figured that had been the reason for him going to the bathroom during group time, to adjust or check his shank and make sure it was ready.

It was fortunate that one of us hadn't been the intended victim. Apparently, knowing who was already in the group, that newer inmate had only joined the group with the specific intention to act precisely as he did. After that, a number of precautions were taken so that similar instances would never happen again.

One part about working in maximum security that I really liked was when I did regular housing reassessments and the inmates scored to advance to medium security housing. For a while, there was the possibility of special reassessments, which were done when housing needed more inmates to move out of max. This is because throughout the prison, inmates causing problems needed to be moved into max, which has limited bed space. Special reassessments had looser criteria and allowed inmates to leave max sooner than if they had to wait to qualify on a regular reassessment.

I frequently checked on all the inmates on my caseload to see if any qualified for the special reassessment. I enjoyed doing things, within policy, that helped inmates. In writing Board reports, I recorded the facts in the computer, such as what working, programming, education, or disciplinaries the inmate had done in prison. Then I would review the report with the inmate and sometimes there were comments, explanations, or "facts" that the inmate wanted included. Then, I would carefully add, "Inmate Smith says that . . ." and include what he said. I learned that I could not record as fact what inmates said, since it was merely their point of view and I didn't know for sure the truth of it.

When I figured the points on the reassessments, I always recorded the source from where the points came. Once in a while, an inmate might claim that something wasn't right, that a previous report was in error, so he didn't think he should have those points for that item on the reassessment. It that case, I would make phone calls and do what I could to verify what he said. I was happy to admit I was wrong and fix things if I could. Usually, inmates would be honest, but there were times when they might make up things, as I found out later when I worked in the intake unit.

I remember comments an inmate made in a group I did with another caseworker with inmates on his caseload. First, we gave strict instructions that no one was to talk to other inmates about anything that was discussed in group. Then we went around the group asking each one to tell some about themselves. One fellow talked about growing up. His mother was gone and he lived with his dad in an apartment. His dad had a girlfriend and then left him at twelve years old to move in with the girlfriend. His dad paid the rent and utilities, and then monthly would give his son some marijuana to sell. When he sold it, then he could buy some food. He was basically provided for, but was still on his own at only twelve years old. Little wonder he was now in prison.

Another fellow, when asked what jobs he had done prior to coming to prison, said that he didn't work. Then he said that he stole, that stealing was his job."

Another inmate's story came to my attention as I read his paperwork. He was born in Iraq. His mother primarily raised him and his eight siblings. He said that after he was born his father left to fight in the Iran-Iraq War. Thereafter, he had no contact with his father until he was ten years old. When he was six years old, he and his sister, who was three years older, were sexually abused. He noted this experience was especially troubling for his sister who committed suicide shortly thereafter. He said that from age nine to ten he was placed in a detention facility for refusing to become a soldier for his native country. At the age of ten, he was a soldier involved in the Persian Gulf War. During this time, he came into contact with his father. He said that during this war he observed his father, brother, and uncle all get killed by gunfire. He also said that he was shot three times in the leg resulting in severe injuries. Thereafter, he was in a prison camp located in Saudi Arabia for four years until he was fourteen years old. He, his mother, and siblings then immigrated to the Utah where they have remained. It is amazing how much this inmate had to endure in his early years.

Another fellow I felt bad for was a guy who had come home and found his wife with another man. He took his gun and shot his wife, not meaning to hit her as she stood in front of her partner. Then there was a fellow in prison who didn't have a criminal history, but had been drinking and driving and killed a person. There was another guy who described what sounded like a reaction to LSD years after he had taken the drug. During that time, he took a crowbar and fatally hit a person over the head. I suppose the majority of the crimes that inmates commit and are sentenced to prison for are related to drugs, either thefts and burglaries to get the money for drugs, possession or distribution of drugs, or crimes done while under the influence of drugs or alcohol.

I enjoyed the story one alcohol drinker told me. He said that he only drank at home, and before drinking he took his keys and pushed them way back under the sofa. After a few drinks he wouldn't be able to find his keys, so he wouldn't be able to drive. Basically, he hid his keys on himself, but later when he sobered up he remembered where he had put them. That was a story I heard outside of prison; apparently his method worked. The whole length of an inmate's sentence is called his expiration date.

The Board of Pardons can choose to terminate an inmate's sentence, so his sentence would be over sooner than the expiration. I was getting gas at a gas station one day upon leaving the prison when I heard my name called. I turned around and saw a man that I didn't recognize. Since I have dealt with a lot of inmates over the years. I didn't remember this one. He explained that he knew me from the prison, so I asked him how he was doing and if he was still on parole. He said no, that his sentence had been terminated. After a pause for a few seconds, when he had apparently been thinking, he said, "That means that we could go out sometime." He knew that staff members were not allowed to socialize with inmates on parole, but it had just dawned on him that he wasn't—that his sentence was over. I was stunned. I didn't know what to say. I didn't want to go out with him. He hadn't actually asked; he had just said that we could. I don't remember what I said to him, but I left as soon as I could.

Chapter THIRTEEN

In September 1972, before we realized that I was expecting our first child, we bought a camper trailer for vacations. Then Susan was born, with Brady coming fifteen and a half months later. Then Don went to work for Vernal City in Utah, so we needed to move. We were having our house built in Vernal, but it wasn't quite finished, so we lived in our camper trailer for three weeks when we moved. Our son was only three months old. After the weeks in the camp trailer, we were able to move into the basement of the house. For a few days that meant washing dishes in a tub. After a few weeks came the carpet on the stairs and on the main level.

Susan was a year and a half old. She had been up to the main level with me, as would sweep and clean up after the workers went home each day. I will never forget that day after the carpet was laid. I took my daughter over to the bottom stair and told her the word carpet as I rubbed my hand over it. She could say carpet. So I encouraged her to crawl up the stairs. Then I heard total pleasure in her little voice as she got to the top of the stairs and looked out over the empty room, fully carpeted and said, "Ah, carpet." We were happy with the carpet too, but we had agreed to do the painting and it wasn't yet done. That was a slow process. We taped a pancake turner with masking tape, then held down each few inches of carpet as we inserted the paintbrush, moving along the walls around the room.

Finally came the day to move up out of the basement into our new home. I don't remember how many weeks or months after that it was that Brady took a crayon or marker to the painted wall near the front door. Knowing that Don would be very upset, I got the paint out and painted over it before Don got home from work. We lived in our Vernal house for about five years. During that time, Don built on the top level with the sloping roof and we had the house plastered, so it looked quite a bit different.

Our next three children, Rebecca, Steven, and Adam, were born there in Vernal. We got our first goats there as well. I was able to be home with my children from the time Susan was born until Steven, the fourth, was about a year old. I would have supper ready when Don got home from work soon after 5:00 p.m. Then I went to work at 6:00 p.m. until 11:30p.m. at the Vernal hospital where I was a nurse's aide. Two weeks after being hired I was able to be in the delivery room, doing whatever the nurse needed. It was thrilling to watch a baby being born. That job only lasted a year because our fifth child, Adam, came, and then I was a patient myself. It was fun being waited on and taken care of by the nurses and aides who I already knew from working there.

While we lived in Vernal, Don and two other guys bought a herd of goats. We got one small male and two or three little female goats. By the next spring, we had offspring and were in the goat milking business. At first, Don did all the milking, both morning and night. After a while, I started milking if Don got up late for work, or was gone on his annual week of business trips. Milking began early in the spring when the little goats were born. Then Don said the goats should be milked in the daylight, so often, I ended up doing it after he left for work. Then he pointed out that it was just about dark by the time he got home in the winter, so could I milk them again before he got home. Susan, Brady, Rebecca, and Steven loved having the goats—when they could help bottle-feed the new little baby goats.

Chapter FOURTEEN

My next years at the prison were spent working in the intake unit. All arriving inmates came through R & O (Reception and Orientation). At first, I did the initial housing assessments on half of all the arriving inmates. Inmates coming to prison for the first time were called New Numbers, probably because they were assigned their prison numbers in chronological order, so their numbers were newer (or larger) than inmates who had arrived days, months, or years before. Doing the initial housing assessment on new numbers meant reading every detail of their crime, since nothing could be copied from a previous assessment. It's hard to imagine some of the horrible things that victims had to go through, particularly in the cases of sex offenders. It was a relief when my job changed to doing the initial assessments on the parole violators.

One amusing situation was when returning to a facility, a parolee was caught during a strip search with a nickel-sized baggie containing a small marijuana cigarette. He refused to admit he put the baggie in his rectum. He claims that he "just tucked it into the back of his pants and doesn't know how it got where it got." It seemed he was trying to explain that he thought it was an ordinary cigarette. Chuckling to myself, I wondered how many normal people would take a partially used cigarette and tuck it into the back of their pants for later use. Inmates will say almost anything in an attempt to avoid guilt.

Another example of innate thinking: Note the excuses that this parole violator comes up with. Below is a segment from a report, with the names left out.

After beating up his wife and calling her a slut (and after being caught) the guy had a drug test. He was positive for methamphetamine. The guy then stated that he had not used meth and could not believe he was positive. He stated that his wife uses meth and she must have planted some in his food or something. Then moments later, he stated that the meth must have come from his coffee pot, because his wife uses the coffee pot for her meth use. He stated maybe he was positive because he kissed her on the mouth after she used some meth.

He requested a second test. It tested positive for meth as well. Sarcastically, he said, "Okay, I used." When given an Admission of Drug Use Form to fill out, he then stated, "This is ridiculous. I'm not signing this; I didn't use." As the agent attempted to take the form from him, he said, "No, I want to sign the form, but first let me tell you why I did." He said he had lead a flawless parole and if it wasn't for his wife he would have completed parole. He also said that Adult Probation and Parole is at fault for making him return home every night (curfew), which forces him to fight with his wife. He blamed his in-laws that they were "garbage people" and that he has never done anything wrong.

Finally, he said, "Well, I'll just go in front of the Board of Pardons and Parole and tell them I'm sorry and get this over with, so I can get back out on parole." He did not sign the form.

How does that sound for not taking responsibility? It didn't seem like he would be changing his ways anytime soon, since it was everyone else's fault and not his. This guy will probably end up with new charges for assaulting his wife, and serve at least a year this time, before he gets out and uses drugs again.

On another day, I did as usual and gave a list of inmates that I needed to see to an officer in order to retrieve them from their cells and bring them in a holding area, where I would take them one by one into my office to interview and for them to sign their initial assessments.

One fellow was brought to my office, cuffed to the chain attached to the wall. I asked his name. He gave a name I didn't recognize. I typed it into the computer to find his inmate number. He gave another name and said that he might be listed that way I still couldn't find him. He proceeded to tell me his story, how he wasn't supposed to be here in Utah in prison. He said he was a federal inmate being transferred from Oklahoma and was supposed to be dropped off in Denver so he could be released, but, for some reason, he said they brought him here to Utah. He didn't know why, but insisted he wasn't supposed to be in prison.

I assumed the housing officers had gotten this fellow out of his cell for me to deal with his situation (along with the rest of the inmates I had on my list to see), since the housing officers wouldn't have known why he was here in prison. The inmate then said that the transporting officers told him that I should just call the Director of Correction, who he mentioned by name, rather than position.

I couldn't understand why he was in our prison if he wasn't a Utah inmate, so I called our records office, explaining that I didn't even know his prison number, and that he wouldn't have one anyway if he had never committed a crime in Utah. The records office, asking if the guy was in my office right then, asked, "So what bed did he sleep in last night?" Checking with the officers, I found what section and what cell he had been in; that led to his correct name, which he hadn't given me. His file was right on my desk. He had been on my list with a regular assessment to sign.

Checking the paperwork in his file, I saw . . . "Mentally Ill." notated. But his story had sounded possible, and he appeared just fine, but none of what he said was true. I was then very glad that I had not called the Director of Corrections, as a mentally ill offender had suggested I do.

Something funny happened the second time I was assigned to the intake unit. It was about three or four months prior that the prison decided to increase security in the intake unit. When inmates arrive at the prison, we classify them with points on a housing assessment document. They are sorted to determine which fellows with a high number of points go to maximum security housing where they are locked in their cells for twenty-three hours a day. Most inmates don't have that many points and so are moved to the main part of the prison where they are out of their cell for most of the day. Before inmates in maximum security (Max) come out of their cell, they are cuffed through the opening where the meals are put through. So the increase in security meant that the officers in intake would always cuff the inmates prior to bringing them out.

I really didn't see much change in the way I dealt with the inmates because it was still possible to sign one's name even with handcuffs on.

Actually, before the change, I used to have to walk an inmate into my office and then cuff one of his hands to a cuff attached to a chain that was bolted to the concrete wall. So the increased security made my job easier because I could now just walk the cuffed inmate into my office.

First, I gave the officers a list of all the inmates that I need to interview that day—the ten, twelve, fifteen, or however many assessments were prepared the day before. Then the officers, with all the cuffs, went to get the inmates from their cells and brought them to a holding area off the main hall in the building. I simply went to the holding area and radioed the officer in the officer's station at the end of the hall to open the holding area door, or "Open Receiving" as we called it. One by one I walked an inmate to my office and explained the assessment and points, got his signature, and then went back to "Receiving" to get the next inmate. I had been doing this same procedure for eight years at that time.

Occasionally an inmate in Receiving will say he needs to use the bathroom. A bathroom is on the other side of the main hall, so it is really close by. An officer might tell an inmate to "hold it" and wait till he gets back to his cell. But I tried to be considerate and helpful when I could. Inmates had to be escorted in our building, so I would stop the interview and let the inmate use the bathroom off the main hall. Usually that bathroom didn't have toilet paper, so I anticipated the need, and said, "Check if there is toilet paper in there, or do you even need paper?" One guy responded that he needed paper, so we walked to the supply room where inmate workers were busy filling intake supply bags, and I got the roll of paper and handed it to the inmate. We then walked back to the bathroom and I figured I'd just stand in the hall nearby and wait.

I turned back to the other inmates in Receiving and explained that I couldn't do any interviews for a few minutes, while I waited for the guy in the bathroom. The inmate, wearing a jumpsuit and cuffs, came out of the bathroom holding the toilet paper with his cuffed hands in the air in front of him, saying, "This won't work."

I felt pretty stupid having expected a cuffed inmate to work with the same ease as an uncuffed inmate had for the last eight years! Because you see, when I had been in the habit of letting the inmates out of Receiving to use that bathroom, it had always worked before the increased security during the last few months.

I carried a cuff key and could have uncuffed him, but might have been told not to by the lieutenant or captain. An officer was nearby and I simply asked him to take the cuffed inmate back to his cell, where he could be uncuffed.

As I turned back to get the next inmate to escort to my office, he said, "I could see that one coming." The other inmates in Receiving had a good chuckle as well.

Needless to say, I laughed at myself for the rest of the day, and even now, when I think about an inmate cuffed and in a jumpsuit, trying to do what was expected.

One day, while an inmate was being transferred from the prison hospital to a larger local hospital, he grabbed a gun and killed the officer guarding him. He ran outside, hijacked a vehicle from a lady just getting out of it, and then was involved in a high speed chase a few miles away ending at a fast-food place where he took hostages. He aimed the gun at one employee, attempted to fire but the gun misfired, and then a customer wrestled him to the ground when the police arrived. If you saw that story on TV, you would remember it, since the inmate had tattoos completely covering his face—really looked ugly if you ask me—he was a gang member, just like his father raised him to be.

The prison was on lockdown for several days afterwards, as prison investigators talked to other inmates of the same gang within the prison. So we, in intake, had our files ready to interview the intake inmates, but couldn't get any inmates out of their cells for a few days. Things did change and we were able to get the signatures on the assessments without going through the cell bars, as would have been the case if they had to stay in their cells longer. The transport officer who died was known by most of us in intake, since he often transported inmates to and from our unit.

It is easy to get complacent and not be as security-minded as one ought to be when working in a prison. Immediately after that incident, security was increased, requiring two officers to transport an inmate out of the prison. Also, more court cases are handled via video so those inmates don't need to be transported.

I worked in intake for eleven years. First, I read the files and figured the points on the assessments, then the next day I met with the inmates to review the assessments, get their signatures, and check the computer to see if they had been referred for county jail housing. The prison had contracts with most of the county jails in the state for additional bed space. Those two days of completing assessments and interviewing inmates were repeated so many times that it began to feel like production work. Once, I counted the number of times an inmate had come to prison—a total of thirteen times, often from parole violations and sometimes with new crimes.

Then came the announcements that there were to be some caseworker transfers. Assigning caseworkers to different caseloads in different housing units wasn't unlike moving inmates around different buildings. One staff member or one inmate might have problems in an area, but then others have to be moved as well in order to fill the vacant spot. I explained that to inmates when they asked why they were being moved—that there was a good chance that they had done nothing wrong, that maybe someone else had.

Chapter FIFTEEN

On December 27, 1980, we moved to West Jordan to the white brick house where we lived for almost twenty years. A few times, I took a goat and a bottle to grammar school for show-and-tell. Susan, Brady, Rebecca, and their classmates really enjoyed seeing the goats. We moved to West Jordan when Susan was in first grade and Brady was in kindergarten. We brought our goats with us when we moved, but had the pig and our rabbits slaughtered. In West Jordan, we raised goats for milk and meat and chickens for eggs.

When Brady was nine years old, another fellow with goats asked if we would care for his goats, and milk them for two or three weeks when he would be on vacation. He offered to pay us. So Don taught Brady how to milk those other goats and he earned the money for it. After that, it became Brady's job to milk our goats, which he did faithfully until Steven was old enough. For a few years, we sold goats' milk and eggs to a few people. To me, that seemed like quite a bother for the little bit that we got paid, but I guess it helped offset the cost of the hay and grain that we bought for the goats and chickens.

Two months after we moved and bought our West Jordan home, we still hadn't sold our Vernal house, so finances were tight. I got a job at the West Jordan Care Center. It is a facility that houses about eighty mentally challenged people ranging in ages from five to sixty. I went to work at 10:00 at night and worked till 6:00 in the morning. During the night, we cleaned and went through two rounds of checking diapers and getting certain residents up to use the toilet. The hardest part was the last hour in the morning. Each of us had the responsibility of getting four residents up, showered, and dressed.

Then it was 6:00 a.m. and I went home and made breakfast and got the children up. After Susan, Brady, and Rebecca were out the door and gone to school, I tried to get a couple hours of sleep. That meant lying down on the floor in front of the bedroom door where Steven and Adam played or slept. After fixing lunch, I would put Adam in his crib and get Steven to lay down with me until the older ones arrived home from school and it was time to start fixing supper. After supper, I was usually able to get another three hours of sleep before it was time to go to work again at 10:00 p.m. I worked weekends and took Wednesday and Thursday nights off, but that job was full time and a challenge with little ones at home during the day.

Then I got pregnant and continued working until a month or so before Carla was born. A year later, I went back to that same job, worked another year, and then had Vanessa. After another year at home, I worked two years until Allison, my eighth and last child, was born. Not ever having morning sickness was a bit of relief trying to work.

During those years, we continued going to church regularly, and I was either a primary teacher or in the nursery. Don was a Cub Master, which involved the whole family. It usually took a day or so to prepare the materials and set up everything at the church in preparation for the monthly Cub Scout pack meeting.

Vacations and trips over those twenty years . . . Don went on yearly one-week business trips, staying in hotels, and eating out. Don would also go on weekend outings, like father-and-son campouts, and several times he took the girls camping for a weekend here or there. During Don's business trips and weekends away with either the boys or girls, I had to be home to take care of the goats.

I remember only five times when I went on trips with him. Two were business trips to Seattle. On one of those trips, I spent the days at a local church member's house, using their computer and typing my genealogy data into the Church's genealogy program.

The other trip to Seattle was when both Don and I had diarrhea and just stayed in the hotel a lot.

Then there was a business trip to Ohio, so I flew to New Hampshire with three little kids to visit my parents; Don came to New Hampshire for the second week. One year we rented a house in Oregon, within walking distance from the ocean. My sister came with us, and Don's parents came for part of that week. I remember collecting starfish and wading in the ocean when the tide was out.

The longest vacation consisted of a three-week driving trip to Yellowstone National Park; to Mount Rushmore; on to Niagara Falls; to Pennsylvania (to meet a third cousin of Don's); to New Hampshire to see my family; to Washington, D.C. (to visit my sister Kathy and her family); to Nauvoo, Illinois; through Kansas (to visit Don's grandmother); to Denver (to visit Don's parents); and finally home. We drove our van—while pulling out camper trailer—with the seat cover pockets and curtains that I made. That was a long way to drive with seven children. It was before Allison was born.

Allison was four and she was the only one home with me when the call came informing me that Dad died. Mom and Dad had bought a house in Florida when they were visiting two of my sisters already living there. Then they were moving to Florida with Mom driving and Dad reading the maps and directing Mom which way to drive. They had driven all the way from New Hampshire to Florida and had gotten into town when Dad asked Mom to pull into the McDonald's since he remembered how convenient their restrooms were for the handicapped. Dad was overweight, previously had had a stroke, had diabetes and used a walker. Dad went into the bathroom and sat down but never came out. After waiting a long time, Mom asked another guy to go in and check on him. He was sitting slumped over, having finished his life on this earth. He had gotten Mom to Florida and could then rest. I cried as I heard the news, then got off the phone and needed to explain to four-year-old Allison what had happened. She was a great comfort to me, even at that tender age.

She was five years old when I got my job at the prison. Don's job with South Salt Lake City had ended and he wasn't able to find another that paid as well, so my job at the prison seemed necessary. I began to feel better about myself; finally, I had a job based on my college education. I had picked any major twenty-one years before, just to graduate, and having a major in Child Development and Family Relations was one of the possible majors toward the Social Service Workers License that I tested for and barely passed.

I applied for a caseworker job at the prison but wasn't hired at first. One of the three people on the interview board was a lady who had worked at a care facility and had wanted to hire me, but was outvoted. She was still interested in me and was going to try to get permission to hire one more person part time, and asked if I would call back in a week. That went on for quite a few weeks, with me checking back every Friday to see if she had it cleared to hire someone part time.

In the spring of 1992, Allison was five when I started my first career job, which was twenty hours a week at the Utah State Prison. For the first two months, I dropped Allison off at a neighbor's and went to work three days a week.

During that summer, my older children were home with the younger ones. Then in the fall, a full-time caseworker position came along. Allison was in school all day and the older children arrived home before the grammar school children did.

Chapter SIXTEEN

About two weeks after hearing there were to be transfers, I received an email that told me where I would be working after the holidays. After seventeen and a half years working in the men's part of the prison, I was to be a caseworker in one of the women's housing units.

I packed my few personal belongings and headed over to my new assignment. I had already received a few emails from my new supervisor, a couple of which concerned two female inmates who were to be released sooner than originally planned. I printed the official Board of Pardons results and decided to give them to those two women as I was leaving my previous unit at the end of the workday the day before Christmas. I stopped at the women's unit to bring one of my few boxes into my new office. Then, locking my new office door, I walked into the common area near some of the cells. Half a dozen women approached me, one or two asking if I was the new caseworker. I said yes, and then added that I needed to see a particular inmate. With the others around, I handed the printed Board results to that woman. She immediately and excitedly exclaimed that she was getting out of prison three months early. A lot of other women joined in her excitement, congratulating her. More gathered around asking if I was the new caseworker.

I walked to another cell and handed the second woman a similar paper with her Board of Pardons results. She was getting out early too. Again, more excitement and more women gathering around. Then someone in the background called out, "What, is everyone getting out early?" Needless to say, I made a good first impression showing up with that good news.

Another situation I remember in those first few weeks was the lady who was pregnant. Her boyfriend was gone and she had gone to prison. She said something about taking the blame for something he had done. She had grown up with mental health issues and had been a real problem for her parents, including victimizing them for money. They were not willing to let her parole to their house. I spent an hour and a half making phone calls trying to find some kind of housing arrangements for this woman who insisted on keeping her baby. She was to be paroled before the baby was born. She could have easily gone to a halfway house, but they would only take her if she had arrangements for someone to care for the baby or if she planned to give up the baby.

I made a list of all the places I called. One would only take women who had been victims of physical abuse in the last month. Another place would only take women needing to detox off of drugs. Another place was a shelter, she would have to get up in the morning and leave and come back at night to sleep there again. It was a day-to-day arrangement. I thought the problem was solved until I spoke to the person who had to approve the parole address—she would not be paroled to a shelter. Her release date was quickly approaching. No solution, so I had to write a report to the Board of Pardons to request that they keep her two weeks longer. A caseworker at the halfway house finally told me that she could parole there for one or two days and they would help her with arrangements to get into some housing where she could have and keep her baby.

I had learned all about the men's intake process over eleven years; now, within in two weeks I had to figure out what to do with a pregnant woman who was getting out of prison. After that, I continued learning the release process. It took a while to catch up. First, I had had to deal with the women who were being released the soonest. Gradually I got organized and was able to start working on release issues ahead of time as they should be done. Besides release issue, there were plenty of other things to do. I had about seven Board reports to process each month. Those are summaries of the working, programming, and disciplinaries that an inmate has received in prison, along with a recommendation to the Board as to when she ought to be released. Housing reassessments also had to be done. They were the same as the initial assessments I had been doing, along with the second column of points to figure in order to determine if the inmates should advance in housing levels.

When I started at the prison, reassessments and Board reports were done from the actual inmate files where all paperwork on that inmate was kept. Usually the files were two or three inches thick. One time, I needed to carry a lot of files to my office to work on. I decided to use my office chair since it would roll along quite nicely. I stacked as many files as I dared on the chair and proceeded to push it through the lobby of the office building. All went well at first, until the pile started to wiggle and shift. The files started to lean and I saw they were about to fall, so I stretched my arms out on each side of the pile of files. That, along with the back of the chair, helped to hold the files in place as I bent over and continued on my journey through the lobby and finally made it to my office.

Now things are different. All the documents in all the files are scanned and can be accessed from any staff computer. Before, caseworkers would submit papers to be manually filed by the secretary. Now, it seems that more tasks have been given to caseworkers to go into multiple programs on the computer and to record data on each inmate.

The women's housing units have caseloads of 144, more than I remember in any of the parts of the prison housing the men. So far, I have kept busy and constantly hope I can get all necessary work done.

Today (note: I write this at home and not during work hours), one female inmate asked, "So do they let you wear that?" referring to what I had on. I would have been quite confused, thinking I was dressed just fine, but she immediately added, "Our visitors can't wear that color." I was wearing a long-sleeved burgundy T-shirt with a short-sleeved white button-up shirt and a burgundy vest with tan pants. Then I realized that she and all the other women were dressed in burgundy scrubs. No one had ever said anything about what colors we were or were not supposed to wear—at least not since the budget cuts, when caseworkers were no longer given uniform allowances. My last comment to her was that I guess I will wear whatever until someone says otherwise. I suppose it would be wise not to go out and buy any burgundy slacks to wear, or staff might notice as well. I soon figured out that the inmate's world is so much of the same day after day, that they notice many more details than the average person might.

That reminds me of another clothing incident that occurred not long after I started working at the prison. Back when we had a clothing allowance, I tried to stay with exactly what I was supposed to wear, basically white or light blue shirts, and navy, tan, or dark gray slacks. One day as I was wearing a light blue shirt and navy pants, I was walking down a long hall in a medium security part of the prison. I was quite a distance away from the control point where the officer sat and controlled the sliding doors in the corridor. The officer was in the habit of only opening the corridor doors for ten minutes per hour when it was movement time for the inmates. I walked up to that corridor door at a non-movement time, expecting it to open immediately. It didn't, and I didn't know why. I just stood there, figuring that the officer was just not paying attention to what he should be doing. Finally, I walked back toward the control point to get his attention to open the door for me. Halfway back the corridor door opened. Then I turned around and headed back to where I was going.

Later, an inmate explained things to me. He pointed out that inmates all wore light blue button-up shirts and blue jeans. I must have looked like an inmate from a distance. But that was what I was supposed to be wearing. The colors for the inmates eventually changed to all white, including white slacks with the word I N M A T E in large letters printed down the front of the leg.

Recently, an inmate, I will call her Jane, finished painting a beautiful tropical waterfall mural on the back wall in my office. She was an older lady with much life experience and many talents.

Among her talents, I would say, was interior decorating. After creating the beautiful mural, Jane suggested to me what else I may have needed in my office to coordinate with the theme of the mural. She said, "Maybe a corn plant, a tall one over there," as she pointed to the corner of my office. I questioned her whether they sell corn plants already grown, or whether I would plant it myself. She explained that it should be tall with wide leaves. It would then match the ferns with the wide leaves in the mural.

Well she was in prison, and couldn't very well go shopping with me to find the right one, so I had an idea. I went to a store that had all sorts of items for decorating. I took my digital camera and took lots of pictures of things I might get for my office, including some dried corn stalks, thinking that at least they had wide leaves. I just couldn't find an already grown corn plant in a pot. I went to work that next Monday and showed Jane the pictures and explained to her that I couldn't find a real corn plant. I told her that I would probably just have to plant a kernel of corn and grow my own corn plant. Jane laughed and said that she meant a "corn-er" plant. Jane talks softly and with her foreign accent, I had completely missed that she had said "corn-er" plant and not corn plant. I felt rather silly at the time, but after a bit more looking, I should be able to find some kind of tall plant with wide leaves already growing in a pot. It seems like inmates always have questions and want to stop in my office to talk. That started on the day I moved to this medium security unit with 144 women. Previously in maximum security and intake, which is part of max, inmates are locked in their cells most of the time, and come to the caseworker's office only when called and are brought in handcuffs. Medium security housing means they are out of their cells a lot of the time with more freedom. Since my office in this women's unit is just off the lobby in the housing unit, women wander over and just stand looking in the window, with a questioning look on their face, "Can I come in?" Often it might start, "I just have a quick question." There are a variety of things they ask: Can you look up an address for me? Can you tell me how much money I have in my account? Can you tell me if I have a date to see the Board of Pardons? I've seen the Board; can you tell me if they have given me a release date yet? I've submitted this phone number, but it doesn't seem to work, can you tell me why? I turned in my Inmate to Inmate Correspondence Request two weeks ago; how long until it will be approved? Is my address approved yet, because I get out soon and don't want to have to go to a halfway house? Can I make a phone call, since my family only has a cell phone and can't accept collect calls?

The first three days working in the medium security women's unit were the worst: a constant barrage of questions all day and paperwork that I knew I needed to get to. I didn't know how I would ever get anything done or be able to do all I was supposed to. Gradually, I learned a few tips from other caseworkers: I needed to establish open-door hours, regular limited times when inmates could stop by and ask questions and other times when my office wasn't "open" for questions.

At first, my open office hours were on Thursdays. That helped, not so many inmates came by, but some still did. I guess I should have turned them away and refused to talk to them until the posted time on Thursday, but that wasn't my nature. I still spoke to them. I would start working on a Board report, only to let myself be interrupted with that questioning face at my window. Whatever the question, it usually meant opening a different program on the computer, rather than the one that I was working on. I would get back to what I was doing, and another inmate would arrive or the phone would ring.

Usually Mondays were the worst. After me being gone for the weekend, the women seemed to come up with lots of questions and things they needed. After a few months of wondering how to get caught up with reassessments and Board reports, it dawned on me . . . make my open-office hours on Mondays, then I would just need to say no, not today, for the rest of the week.

Time has passed and Mondays seem to work better for open office hours. This week I had another problem; it seems that Inmate Accounting somehow missed sending out the regular statements to everyone in our building, so I called them and explained that several inmates in our building had talked to others living in other units, who received their statements. Inmate Accounting said they would reprint the statements and send them out.

Chapter SEVENTEEN

I TALKED TO MY husband Don about my belief that Bill was wrongly convicted. I had some paperwork that Bill gave me that I asked Don to read. Don did not want to bother; a movie was on TV that he wanted to see. I talked to my supervisor at work about my belief in Bill's innocence. I was given a book to read, *Games that Convicts Play* and had to write a report on it. The book told about how inmates try to deceive you, little by little.

No one wanted to deal with the possibility that an innocent man was in prison! There were details too numerous to mention that made it clear to me that Bill was indeed innocent. I talked to another caseworker, Laddie, because he knew Bill. He listened as I told him a lot of things about Bill's case.

The days and weeks and months went on. I talked to Bill. I read his file. I talked to Laddie. He listened and knew that I believed Bill was innocent. He did not tell me his opinion about Bill, but it was good to have someone to talk to. I should have been able to talk to Don about my belief in Bill and how he was convicted. I had tried, but he didn't want to hear it. To me, it was so much more important than any TV show, that an innocent man was in prison. I could never understand why Don wasn't interested in something so important to me. I had tried to help Bill with his case in ways that I could, even breaking some prison rules. That just led to me losing a week's worth of vacation time/pay, rather than being suspended for a week and having to stay home. Eventually Bill paroled after fifteen years.

A couple years after trying to talk to Don about Bill, Don called my attention to a prison story on the news where some inmate in another state who had been in prison for four years had his case overturned and he was released. I was so upset at Don, that he would believe a story on TV about a man being wrongly convicted, when Don would not believe me and acted like he didn't care when I said the same thing about an inmate I was responsible for on my caseload.

It was not always easy, my life at home with eight children, then going to work full time. My two lives seemed so different. At home, I cooked, cleaned, did laundry, and things that I thought I should do to be a good mother. Once I got home from work—and no sooner did I walk through the front door—three separate conversations with me began. Two children, at the same time, along with Don, were trying to tell me things that had happened with them or what they needed me to do. My goal was to get through all this and get started on the meal, so I glanced at one of them for a second or two, then made eye contact with the next, and finally looked at the third person. All three continued talking to me. Needless to say, I felt responsible to listen, to be there, and to do what I could for Don and for the kids.

Work was a different feeling. I felt important. I wrote Board reports, gave recommendations to the Board of Pardons and Parole when the inmates ought to be released within the parameters set by the courts. At that time, I wrote my reports in longhand, and one of the secretaries typed them. There were male caseworkers and female caseworkers doing the same job. I did a job equal to men who supported their families. I felt good about myself. In fact, one of the secretaries was even a man.

It was at about that same time that my sister and I started going to Weight-Watchers. After a slow start, I lost fifteen pounds, then another fifteen pounds in the next few months. At work, people started to notice. Inmates, as well as other staff, complimented me on how good I looked. It was like a sense of euphoria (opposite of depression); I loved my job. I felt important. It was springtime and beautiful outside. I was wide awake and no longer working graveyard. The flowers smelled so good. People continued telling me how good I looked. I felt like I was on top of the world—like I could do anything.

It was in that setting that my emotions overtook reason, and I fell. I was unfaithful. I immediately went to the Bishop because I had done things I never would have thought that I could or would ever do. I tried to start on the right road again. The Bishop became sick for quite a while, and I felt so alone. I was excommunicated as part of the process of repentance. Talks at home with my husband always became arguments. Within a year or so, we started going to marriage counseling. Time passed. My life continued.

I wanted things to get better. I continued going to Church as I always had. I knew the Church was true. There were so many things to deal with. I felt stuck. My job was important. I thought we needed the money. I liked my work and wanted to keep my job. Altogether, I think we went to four different marriage counselors over a four-and-a-half-year period.

Susan, the oldest, was married by then but would often come to visit and talk to her dad and me. She knew us both, and did her very best in trying to help us work things out.

Then came that fateful day—October 4, 1997. Susan was six and-a half-months pregnant with her third child, a boy, and had two daughters, ages six and four. On that fateful day, she was in a car accident. An emergency C-section was done in Cedar City before Susan and the baby were life-flighted to Salt Lake City. Susan was unconscious for two days until she died. After that, I started picking up my two little granddaughters every Friday afternoon. That was what Susan would have wanted me to do. Allison was still short enough to play on the equipment at the fast-food places we often went to with her two little nieces. The new little baby boy was in intensive care at Primary Children's Hospital for two months. When he was a year old, I included him every Friday and picked up all three grandchildren to spend time with them.

I had dreams about Susan the first few months after she was gone. The first one was of Susan and me. We were just sitting and talking, as we often had in life. Susan stood up, as if to leave, and started walking away. Just at that moment in the dream, I was aware of the unique opportunity I had had, being able to see and talk to her, because I knew Susan was no longer alive, so I spoke to her as she walked away. Calling her by name, I said, "Susan, I love you! I just want you to know I love you." As soon as I spoke, Susan started running away. I knew she had heard me since she no longer walked away, she ran, but could not stay. Then I awoke from the dream, and knew that Susan knew that I loved her.

In another dream, I remember seeing Susan, and I reached out and touched her on the knee, and I knew Susan was real. In the last dream, I was sleeping in my bedroom downstairs; I was able to ask Susan three questions. "Where are you?" Susan held her hands just above her shoulders with fingers extended and slightly away from her body, saying, "Just around," giving me the idea that she was just around the area I was in. The second question I asked Susan in the dream was, "What do you do?"

Susan said, "Soothing to eleven." I took that to mean that she comforted people, possibly eleven people. The third question I asked Susan in the dream was, "Will I see you again?"

Susan answered, "In six weeks." I awoke and marked down the day it would be in exactly six weeks. When the time came, I didn't remember that was the night that I was supposed to see Susan again. Don and I had argued that evening, and then I went to bed. The next morning, I remembered, and realized that I hadn't seen my daughter—probably because of the argument, and not having the right spirit when I went to sleep.

After four years of spending time with my grandkids every Friday, my son-in-law and his new wife asked if I would mind cutting it down to every other Friday, since that would fit better with his wife's ex-husband picking up his three kids every other weekend. So that is what I did.

Allison and I would often take the three grandchildren and go visit her married sister, Rebecca, and her three boys every other Friday afternoon. Those were fun times with two of my daughters and six grandchildren. We would go to parks with food we brought and they could play on the swings, slides, and monkey bars.

Chapter EIGHTEEN

Our housing unit, for which I am the caseworker, has four sections each with nine cells upstairs and nine cells on the main level, and each cell houses two inmates. That means 144 women for me to deal with. That might be too much to deal with, given the fact that women seem to be needier than men, but some women inmates are used as "Leads" over the other women. There is one head lead, with two assistant leads over the four sections. Each section has a lead with an assistant lead and quite a few specialized leads are in each section. To name a few, one is a "Feel Good" lead, and it is pretty obvious what her job is to do for the others. There is a literacy lead who posts all bulletins and information. One is assigned to keep track of volunteer service hours; all the inmates are encouraged to do volunteer hours. Some inmates have access to a computer to use for community purposes, but not for personal use. One such inmate offered to come up with a schedule and print for me which sections of inmates had access to my open-office hours during which time of day, also allotting a separate time for those that worked all day, like kitchen and commissary workers.

I'm still trying to learn about the privilege level system. When inmates first arrive at our unit, they start at a lower level. After orientation, they move to the next level. After different amounts of time and receiving no disciplinary write-ups and no negative chronological notes, they can earn higher levels with more privileges, like longer out-of-cell time and the ability to buy more commissary, and increased visiting times.

Learning the system is one thing, but I prefer the interaction with people. There are rules for visiting and getting people approved to be on the inmate's visiting list. The other day I came up against a unique situation. The inmate was having difficulty getting her mother approved to visit. She hadn't seen her in seven months. The problem was that her mother worked at the prison.

It would jeopardize an inmate's safety for other inmates to know that she had a special relationship with a staff member. Force or intimidation might be used. It was originally arranged under special circumstances and with verbal permission, but then came a number of staff transfers. The inmate was then told that her visit was not going to happen. She came to me to explain that she needed to discuss her release plans, whether or not she was going to live with her mother when she got out of prison.

Writing letters is a valid form of communication, and maybe I should have told her that is what she would have to do. Instead, I considered that a phone call would better meet her needs; also, verbal permission had originally been given for a special visit. I arranged for a time to call the cell phone number of the staff member at a time when she would be off duty. At the appointed time, and with the inmate in my office, we called the number. The number didn't work. After more time and more phone calls to others, we found the correct number and that inmate was finally able to talk to her mother.

I felt like an intruder, but security demanded that I remain in the office while the phone call took place. After loving words and some things she laughed about, she got to the point, saying how much she wanted to come home to her mother when she was released, but she was tired of coming back to prison and thought it would be best to do something different this time. She was pleased when her mother agreed that she should live with another relative in another neighborhood.

When doing paperwork, working with inmates and writing reports for the Board of Pardons, presentence investigation reports are always in the inmate files. As a caseworker, I often read the presentence reports. One part is the life history section, a brief summary of the person's life. Often in public, when I interact with people outside of prison, I sometimes wish I could read a presentence report on those people. How great that would be in making life-changing decisions or in advising a child about the friends they keep.

Today was the first day back to work after a trip visiting two of my sisters in Florida. One sister was babysitting her first granddaughter, and it was easy to see her love as she doted over the toddler for two days and two nights as we visited with her.

Then coming in to work, I heard, "Hi, caseworker," from across the large grassy area as I walked the long sidewalk approaching the building of 144 women for which I provide caseworker services. Half a dozen women were sitting on the grass besides the building behind the wire fence that segregated their section of the outdoors from others. After the greeting, I waved and then I heard, "We've been waiting for you." That made me feel quite welcome after being gone a whole week.

I got settled in and proceeded with a week's worth of email and finally to some reassessments I had to do. One reassessment was being done to justify the move of a woman to maximum security housing. There had been an incident, a sexual assault on another woman, while I had been gone. She had been immediately moved to another building that houses the women's maximum security inmates. Figuring the number of points for the assessment involved reading the inmate's paperwork, including information about her original crime. The original crime followed a second marriage in which she had been a victim of physical violence. The violence had been ongoing for months, including threats on her, her family, and her little daughter. Then the "discipline" started on the little child, for which a variety of objects were used to discipline the child. The mother was threatened and intimidated, so she disciplined her little daughter as well. First it caused welts, then scabs and more welts, and finally puss. Besides the hitting, alcohol and other things were applied to "heal" the many sores on the little body; the ointments were intended to burn and continue the discipline process. After a few months, the little toddler was blessed to be able to die and have an end to the torture she had been enduring.

Why is one child so blessed to have parents, grandparents, aunts and uncles all doting on her every need and another child have to endure so much physical pain from those who are supposed to love her? Prison is intended to restrict an inmate's freedom, but the necessities of life are guaranteed. How much better treatment are the perpetrators receiving from the state than the little victim received from her mother and stepfather? Life just isn't fair.

Chapter NINETEEN

I THINK IT WAS Easter of 1999 when I got unique Easter baskets for each of my children—glass banana split dishes. For Easter, they had candy in them, but afterwards, we used them for banana splits, usually on Sunday afternoons. One Sunday, Brady visited with his family, commented that he was hungry and asked if he could he have something to eat before the ice cream. That started my Sunday Family Dinners, since Brady and Rebecca had moved out by then. Eventually, dinner every Sunday changed to every other Friday night.

To continue the story of Don and me, I kept on trying to talk to him, to explain how I had not meant to hurt him and how I was so sorry, and how I wanted his forgiveness. A few years passed. I was happy when I could serve others since I didn't have an official calling in the Church. I watched the choir director's son on Sunday afternoons, and the bishop's daughter when his wife taught Sunday School.

The Church got a new bishop. I talked to him, and Don and I both talked to the new stake president. Life continued with us living in the same house. Eventually the bishop and stake president agreed that I could be rebaptized. It was 1998, and I was thrilled to be a member again. Over the years, it had seemed that every Church sermon (talks given by members, requested by the bishop or his two counselors) and every song was directed straight at me about what I wasn't included in. Don was sitting in the back of the small group that attended my baptism. Once it was over, he immediately got up and left without speaking to anyone. That was how the next four months went; he spoke to me as little as possible. We lived in the same house, and I took care of the kids as I always had. Don chose to fix his own meals and bought his own food, which he kept in a couple of small refrigerators in his room.

I wanted to look forward to the day when I could go to the Temple to do Susan's work. She had been baptized during life, but she had not had her marriage sealed in the Temple for eternity. However, I did not see any way I could ever get a Temple Recommend again to go to the Temple with my strained marital relationship. Supposedly Don had not done anything serious enough to lose his Temple Recommend. He recognized his emotional abuse in marriage counseling, but he would not admit it to the Bishop. I had sinned, I had repented, but Don would not speak to me after my re-baptism. It was as if he couldn't forgive me. In the Temple Recommend interview, I would not be able to answer questions about a good relationship and support for my husband as a Priesthood holder, so I filed for divorce. Then the custody battle began. The custody evaluator came to the house and interviewed Adam, Carla, Vanessa, and Allison. Adam was over eighteen. Allison was clear in her wishes about wanting to live with me.

The recommendation came back that Carla, Vanessa, and Allison should not be separated, so the judgement would likely be in Don's favor. The children heard Don say more than once that if I wanted out, I should just leave, giving them the idea that Don would be the one getting the house. I believe that the children just wanted to stay near their friends, and not have to choose between their parents. My attorney suggested that we settle so that Carla and Vanessa would be able to stay in the house with their dad and be near their friends, and that we would have joint custody of Allison, who would live with me, which she did from the beginning. I did not want to fight him for the house, the yardwork, the detached garage, and all the old furniture. Our divorce was final April 6, 2000.

In March, Allison and I moved into an apartment on the same street. I had paid the rent for four months already so I would have a place ready when things had settled. Allison and I lived in the apartment from March 2000 to February 2001. It was a real relief, living in my own place. It was calm in the evenings when I got home from work, with just Allison and me. A lot of times, we went out for fast food. I still had my family dinners in my apartment. The kids and grandkids would come over on Sundays. The only problem was . . . no dishwasher in the apartment.

In December, I received my equity settlement and started thinking about what and where I wanted to buy to live in. I called a real estate agent I knew, and she showed me a half dozen houses. I couldn't decide. I didn't really want to move out of the neighborhood I had lived in for twenty years. I was sitting at work one day, doing paperwork, and thinking that if I bought one of the houses I looked at, the thirteen-year-old Allison would come home from school, be by herself, and not know anyone in the neighborhood. All of a sudden, it dawned on me! I knew I wanted to buy one of the four townhome units in the brand-new building at the end of the same street where Don's house and the apartment were. Immediately I called the real estate agent and told her my decision to buy the townhome in West Jordan, Utah.

Chapter TWENTY

TODAY WAS A BETTER day. I had seven Board reports to do for the month, but I didn't have time to do them before my vacation. Today I finished them—such a good feeling. Then I got my next monthly lists: nineteen reassessments to do and I think it was nine more Board reports. This month I will have more time for work since my vacation is over.

One funny thing happened, and as a result, I will probably have more uninterrupted time to do my work. It had to do with boundaries, my boundaries, or lack thereof. Actually, Boundaries is one of the life skills classes that inmates take. Maybe that's it . . . maybe the inmates are learning about boundaries and using it against me. Anyway, I have one day a week set aside when my 144 female inmates are able to sign a list and come to my office for their issue or question or problem. Lately that day has been on Mondays.

After my vacation, I flew into town on Monday, and got back to work Tuesday of this week. Some inmates couldn't wait until next Monday and came to my office and just stood outside of the window, waiting and watching to see if I would motion for them to enter. Guess what? I did. I answered a number of questions and sent all but one on her way. The last one apologized for bugging me on a day other than Monday. She wanted to help me deal with inmates coming and standing at my window, so she said she would go and talk to the "Lead" inmate with some ideas. I didn't think anything about it until I was leaving and the Lead inmate approached me. All of a sudden, I remembered a previous talk I had had with the Lead inmate, who had suggested that I simply lock my office door and have a sign-up list for Mondays, so that my days would be more orderly. I had violated what I had told her I would do. So there I was, apologizing to the Lead inmate for helping those other inmates when it wasn't scheduled. I admitted my own problem with boundaries and thanked her for helping and promised to keep my door locked except on Mondays.

Having Lead inmates over the other inmates seems to work with women, but would never have worked in the men's housing units. Male inmates are competitive and worry about their image. Female inmates act more like sisters and often tell all their "stuff" to each other. I don't think the males share so many personal details. Male inmates seemed to like to play head games, creating situations, like telling one person something and then telling another person something different so those two eventually have a problem with each other. Then the person instigating the trouble would just sit back and observe what happened. The plan would be that the instigator doesn't get into trouble but enjoys watching others get into trouble or fight. I worked eleven years in the men's intake unit and those sorts of head games passed the time and worked better on the "fish," as the new inmates entering prison were called.

As more and more people use cell phones now, inmates are less able to call family or friends, since cell phone numbers cannot be approved and be placed on their phone list. Consequently, caseworkers get all kinds of requests from inmates to be able to call on staff phones. A lot are denied. But yesterday there was one. The inmate was honest enough to admit that she had already been allowed to call her grandmother by a correctional officer (before she would be asking me for a call) when her three-year-old had an accident a few days prior. She started by explaining that she was going to be in prison long enough that her son, who was in foster care, would be adopted. The three-year-old was being cared for at the inmate's grandmother's house. It so happens that the grandmother had been an emergency room nurse and knew what to do and reacted immediately.

The little boy was playing across the street and went into the house when the six-year-old and a couple others were outside. The three-year-old climbed up and looked out the window and saw the opened jackknife laying in the windowsill where the six-year-old had left it. As the three-year-old was climbing down with the knife in his hand, it somehow got jabbed into the white of his eye. He pulled it out, and then screamed.

The inmate was given the use of a staff phone to call a few days before by a housing officer and knew that her child had been immediately taken to the hospital by the grandmother and that he was initially okay. She wanted an update of his condition. Since the inmate had already been given a phone call about this and since it really wasn't an emergency now, I told her that I would make a quick call just for an update of his condition but not let her have a second phone call for that incident. The inmate was relieved to find out that the little fella could still see and seemed to have perfect vision in that eye.

Over the years, I have learned that when I allow an inmate a phone call about one issue, it could and often would turn into many other issues, such as a guy in prison would want to know if the girl he was seeing was going to stick with him while he was away. But he knew that asking for a phone call for that reason wouldn't work, so it was always because of a family member with some serious medical situation. That would be the first five minutes, asking how the person was, then the conversation would continue for as long as possible, but in a lowered voice. It always amazed me how, sitting in the same room, I couldn't hear most of what was said, but apparently the person on the other end of the phone could. Today I had a rare opportunity. As a post-certified staff, I was the one to provide security for two college students who were to interview a female offender. They were studying depression related to adoption. They questioned and this Latter-day Saint inmate told her story. First, she was a victim and endured much abuse from her stepfather until eight years old. Then, she stood up to the man and threatened to tell what he had done if he didn't stop. He stopped, but later she did tell anyway and he spent time in prison. She grew up, married, and had one child. No more children came for a while, so she adopted a child. The adopted child had behavioral problems.

There were issues about the child that she wasn't told prior to the adoption. She continued with the story of having the adopted child sealed to her and her husband in the LDS Temple so the adopted child would belong to her and her family in Eternity. She told of her feelings and spiritual experiences concerning the child, and how much her faith helped as she went through struggles with the adopted child. The inmate said how she didn't feel very good about herself, and over time she learned that she had to forgive the person who had offended against her in order to be able to love herself.

That lady has been in prison for a number of years now, having caused the death of another person. She has taken many classes and now teaches others what she has learned. She is a leader among the inmates and sets a good example of how to follow the rules and isn't afraid of challenging others as they break the rules.

Working in the prison gives me the feeling of helping. I am paid to write reports—Board reports to recommend when inmates should be released. A few days ago, an inmate heard bad news, her medical results . . . her cancer had come back. She had remaining probably only a few months. She had a year left on her sentence. I wrote the report asking for immediate release, so she could go home to another state to spend her remaining weeks with her family. Her family will be taking care of her, no more risk that she will be doing any more thefts. She won't have the strength with the chemotherapy that she will be undergoing. She said she plans to fight it, the cancer, but there really wasn't much hope. She has basic Christian beliefs, so I told her what I believe, about death being like a doorway. First, we are here in this "room," then, in an instant, we go through death, and we are over there in the other "room" and everything is fine. No pain, no suffering afterwards. Just as a person doesn't usually hang around in a doorway, we don't linger in the process of death. It is over in an instant.

Another experience of death was told to me by a family member. She was with a grandmother who wasn't feeling well and was lying down in bed. When her time came, she raised her head and looked around the room near the ceiling, and then laid her head down and that was it. No doubt was in the mind of the person viewing the event that the grandmother had seen previously departed loved ones who had come for her, probably even her beloved husband. Death happens in an instant and is nothing to be feared, as experienced by this grandmother.

Chapter TWENTY-ONE

BUYING MY FIRST HOME felt really good—just as it had when buying my first car—after being married almost thirty years. Allison and I were excited and happy to move into our new place. Moving into the apartment was mainly a matter of buying my furniture and washer and dryer and having it all delivered to the apartment. I only took my clothes and the small TV and small microwave when I moved out of Don's. Moving from the apartment to my townhome a year later was a bigger project. I got lots of boxes and had them all packed and ready when Saturday morning came. About ten or twelve neighborhood members from Church came to help. It was a miracle how everything was moved in only one hour, furniture and everything, including having the washer and dryer hooked up. Everyone helped and carried my stuff out of the apartment, walking past the next apartment building and into the townhome. I remember sleeping my first night there; I woke up on Valentine's morning and it seemed like it was still a dream, hard to believe that I could really stay in that beautiful brand-new place, that it was really mine!

Carla went away to college, so after a year with Don, Vanessa moved in with me and Allison, and eventually Adam did too. Vanessa's move was against the custody agreement, but Don did not fight it. Don did not insist that Allison go back and forth and stay half the time with him. Carla was then over eighteen. The attorney said I had to wait three months when Vanessa moved in with me; she could just as easily move back, but she didn't in those three months, so I went back to court and got full custody of Vanessa and Allison. I originally lost the custody battle, but I felt very blessed to have the other children with me after that one year.

As soon as my divorce was final, I started going to singles activities. I went on several hikes, a few dinners, and a number of dances. I wanted very much to find someone. My sister, who was not married, and I went to several singles conferences together.

Don was married two and a half months after our divorce was final. I tried the online singles thing. One fellow I met and had lunch with turned out to be married; I called to thank him for lunch . . . his wife answered the phone. Why would he give me his phone number at lunch and then leave the phone home with his wife when he went out of town that afternoon for his trucking job? Maybe that had something to do with what he explained to me about how you could call a number, enter some info, and have the phone call connected though the computer and Internet. Well that didn't work for me when I tried it, so I just called his cell phone directly. When his wife answered, I apologized and said that I would never bother either of them again.

Then there were the two other fellows, each of whom I dated a few times. They dumped me as their second choices as each had been dating another woman whom they soon married. About a year later, I heard that both were again divorced. That could have been me. I figured the heavens were watching over me during that time.

The last online guy that I almost went out with admitted that he was actually ten years older than what he had listed on his profile. Hmm, looking back I should have quit right then. We continued to "chat" via the computer as was the custom before texting came along. Finally came another admission. He was on probation for a sex crime against a child. So I asked, "Isn't it against your probation rules to date a woman with a minor child at home?" I knew it would have been against the rules for a parolee (who had been in prison for a sex crime against a child) to date someone with a minor child. He said no, that it was okay. But it wasn't okay for me, due to my job and the fact that my youngest was still twelve years old. Plus, I remembered how he lied about his age, so I never even met him.

Knowing I could support myself financially felt good, and in time I came to realize that it would be okay if I was to stay single. I felt blessed to have the children and grandchildren that I did. My oldest, Susan, was never far away when I picked up her children and spent time with them. I was happy that Brady had found his wife and that they had four girls.

Rebecca is a good mother to her three boys and was a good caretaker for her husband's grandmother when she lived with them. I was glad when

Steven met his wife, and happy when they got married. Both seem to be doing well in their careers. I liked my Adam's red-haired friend, but that wasn't to be. I am glad he has found his place as a professional chef. Carla found her match, and they seem good together; both have been a great help to me. They are good parents to their three little ones. Vanessa made a good choice with her fellow. They have three boys so far. Allison seems happy with her husband and their little boy and girl. I am grateful for and very proud of all of my children and the good choices they have made in their lives.

I have always believed in and attended Church. Finally, in 2003 I was able to get my Temple blessings restored. I will never forget the warmth that I felt surged throughout when I first put on my temple garments after so long without wearing them. While I was living those years (2001 to 2004) in the townhome and Mom was living in Florida, she often called to talk. I would tell Mom about visiting Rebecca and what interesting things her three boys and their grandma were doing. Then I told her about a house that was for sale across the street from Rebecca's in Magna. Later, Mom said that she was moving to Utah and would be here before winter. I was living as a divorced person, still in Don's neighborhood.

In the townhome, I had three bedrooms with three children living with me. Allison only had one more year of high school. Either Mom could buy the Magna house and I would continue driving to Magna to visit Rebecca and Mom, or I could buy the house and Mom could live with me. I chose the latter option. That gave me four bedrooms. I thoroughly enjoyed those four years being able to see Rebecca's family more often. It also worked out for Rebecca, that Mom was there for her boys when they got home from school while she was at work. Mom enjoyed gardening and bought a red wagon instead of a wheelbarrow.

My grandsons loved taking things apart and building other things, so part of the wagon got reused in a go-cart. They seemed to forget that they agreed to put the wagon back together before school started again. I'm not sure if it was for the go-cart or for another one of their projects that they harvested nails from my wood fence. When I saw them standing on the cross board on the fence and leaning over it, and doing the same thing in a number of different spots on the fence, I asked what they were doing. I was told that each board in the fence had three nails and they were only taking one out of each. I said no, no more. How could I be upset at them? They helped me with many tasks such as snow shoveling, weed eating, vacuuming, cleaning my car, putting up my Christmas tree, outdoor lighting, and any job I could think of.

My job at the prison continued. I had met Laddie when I started working at the prison in 1992. He was also a caseworker and often helped me as I learned about inmates and what the job involved. I'll never forget the staff meeting to which he brought the large turtle for show-and-tell. He talked about the turtle to everyone's amusement. Everyone liked Laddie, inmates and staff.

Once, our supervisor invited all caseworkers and their spouses out to eat. At the restaurant in 1993 or 1994, Don got to talking to Laddie about camping. They decided on a camping trip to Capitol Reef. We went. I remember how windy it was. The next morning, Laddie announced that he wanted to go for a hike. His twelve-year-old son wanted to go too. His wife didn't want to go and Don didn't want to go, but I did. So we went for a hike, Laddie, his walking stick, his son, and me. In 1995, Laddie transferred to work at the prison in Gunnison. A year or two later we, the caseworkers, each got our own computers and then had the Internet and email. We could email each other. At first, it was often, the months went by until I would hear from Laddie about some computer or inmate question. Often he would ask how my family was doing. I told Laddie about things in my life: Susan dying and my divorce. I told Laddie about picking up and spending time with my three grandkids.

Chapter TWENTY-TWO

I GOT BACK TO work after a week's vacation. There to greet me at my office was my supervisor. He explained that I was being transferred. After less than a year in the women's housing unit, I was to be moved to the women's unit that houses the intake, maximum security, and the mental health female inmates. I wasn't asked, and usually don't like change, but like the inmates, I usually do what I am told. Later, I realized that my supervisor had to tell me immediately when I walked in that morning, or I might have read it in the meeting minutes of the staff meeting from two days earlier. During my absence, it had been announced that another caseworker and I would be trading assignments. Like it or not, I was to leave these ladies that I had come to know and was comfortable working with. Rose, who painted the beautiful tropical waterfall mural on my office wall, had been moved out of my unit. I was sad that I would not be able to take that mural with me when I moved to my new office in the other unit. I knew that maximum security inmates, mental health inmates, and intake inmates would not be out of their cells for sufficient time each day to be able to paint as the medium security inmates had been.

I happened to mention to the lead inmate that I wouldn't be able to take my mural with me. She simply said that inmates could go over to that unit to paint, even if they didn't live in that unit. Life goes on. I just needed to find another picture for that office.

My move wasn't to take place until after a week after Thanksgiving. On the day before Thanksgiving, I walked into my office to find six inmates sitting around the table in the lobby just outside of my office.

Spread on the table was an assortment of candy, yarn, and silver bags. I asked what they were doing. They said they were making Thanksgiving gifts for all of the thirty-six women in their section. Some didn't have money to buy things from commissary, but they wanted to do something for all of them.

One must remain constantly suspicious of things in a prison, so I asked, "Where did you get that stuff?" I knew they could purchase candy and yarn, but I was curious about the little silver bags. One lady took a bag and showed me the inside. It was an individual serving Nachos bag turned inside out. She explained that when meals are served with useful items, then she just collects them from everyone. I have seen male inmates collect corn dog sticks and make use of them.

I unlocked my office door and proceeded to turn my computer on. A few minutes later there was no need for her to knock, since I could plainly see through the large windows in my office that she wanted something. She had a little silver bag for me, bulging and tied with a blue piece of yarn. She said it was for me and that they were sorry to lose me as a caseworker. I took the bag home and opened it. What a treasure and sacrifice to receive such a gift from people earning only forty cents an hour! Purchasing their bags of taffy and hard candy to share with others was more expensive to them and much more of a treasure than that of a person outside of prison buying the same items.

In that office with my beautiful waterfall mural, I had my half frig and my microwave. A couple of years before, I had received an email announcing to all prison employees that a small refrigerator was available for use at work, so I immediately responded and went over to the other building on prison property to see what it looked like. It looked used, but it worked. Suspiciously, I asked about it, wondering what it had been used for. My son Steven was the person offering it. He assured me that it had only been used for medications but never urine samples.

I was and am proud of Steven for following in my footsteps in his career choice, not as a caseworker, but still working with inmates. Anyway, getting back to the frig, he was happy to load my little frig on the handcart that we found. He rolled my frig out of that building and down the sidewalk and into the other complex where my office was. Never once did he say anything about how he felt. Later, I learned that he had been in pain all weekend, but had still come to work. Finally the office manager insisted that he go home. So he moved my little frig about noon and then was in the hospital before the end of the day, with surgery scheduled the next day.

Having that frig worked fine for a while, then the secretaries started putting their food in it too. It was, after all, closer to their offices than the full-sized frig that was across the lobby at the other corner of the building. Then one day, someone switched frigs. The full-sized frig was moved into the large office I shared with another caseworker and the little frig that I laid claim to (as much as one can claim state property) was moved to that out-of-the-way storage room where the big frig had been. That worked out perfectly the day I was reassigned to work in the women's part of the prison. My little frig was no longer used by anyone else, I was completely free to take it with me when I moved.

Having a frig, I knew I also needed a microwave in my office. When I had started working at the prison, staff could eat meals at the prison free of charge. Over the years, things changed, and we had to order ahead and pay to eat prison meals. It was simple to go to a store and buy a small microwave. Bringing it into the prison was another story. I had to let it sit and wait until a clearance was done. A few days later, I was able to bring it to my office. It sat perfectly right on top of the frig. I would buy a week's supply of microwave meals and bring them with me at the beginning of each week, and I was set for lunch. It was also necessary to bring water bottles. We used to have water coolers with the upside down jugs—again budget cuts.

Lunch worked out fine that year. It was then that the Hard Times Café opened. It was on prison property along the frontage road. I went over there for lunch and found I liked it, good prices and freshly made deli sandwiches and soup. I never bought the hamburgers and fries. Male inmates worked there cooking and preparing the food. But guess what? No inmates ever worked at the cash register. Female civilians were hired for that. It worked pretty well. It did get pretty busy at lunchtime, as they would take delivery orders as well as serving customers who walked in. Food was delivered to all parts of the prison since most officers weren't allowed to leave their housing units. Recently, they had a contest to rename the Hard Times Café. My suggestion was "Stars 'n Bars," but whoever did the judging liked "Serving Time Café," and that became the new name of the café. The public is welcome to stop in for breakfasts and lunches. Then it was time, so I moved out of my waterfall mural office and into my office in the unit housing the female intakes, maximum security, and mental health ladies. The walls in that office were solid colored and plain. That was okay, because I was so busy with paperwork. The previous caseworker would give the officers a list of the inmates she needed brought to her office to sign their initial housing assessments. I knew that was the best way, but it took longer. I did it once and I found myself spending too long talking to each lady. For some reason, that had never been a problem when I worked intake in the men's unit. My solution was to do all my assessments and then walk around to each cell, since intake inmates are "at home" twenty-three hours out of every day. In medium security housing they can be out of their cells most of the day. I would simply slide the assessment under the door and they could look it over and ask any questions and then sign it and slide it back. That way took only a few minutes and seemed to work better for me.

Chapter TWENTY-THREE

It was on a Saturday night while living in Magna, when I got a phone call after forty years, from my former missionary. I was single, and it was great to his voice again, but he was married. His wife was on the line too. They wanted me to visit them where they lived an hour and a half away. I still like him and was excited to see him again after all those years and wanted to meet his wife. I wanted to look good, and so I got a perm one week before the appointed time to see them. That was a mistake; my hair was frizzy and funny on that breezy day. We took turns riding their horses and visited most of the day. They asked me to come visit again and again, so once a month, I drove the hour and half and enjoyed the time I spent with them.

His wife was always there and the three of us became very good friends. They believed that the Second Coming wasn't very far away, and that plural marriage would again be practiced and legal in the country and in the Church. Over the next four years I continued visiting with them. I wondered a bit about how soon the Second Coming would really be. I made it clear that I believed strictly in what was currently preached and practiced and that I wouldn't be involved in any plural marriage unless the LDS Church and the laws of the land permitted it.

Mom was living with me and went a few times with me to visit my missionary and his wife for those years. Mom helped me deal with my life as a single person. Visiting regularly with Susan's children had tapered off as my grandson would choose to spend his time with Rebecca's son, his cousin, and the two granddaughters chose to be with their friends or worked. I loved them and was glad for the times we had together during my efforts to deal with the loss of my daughter.

Then Mom decided to move back to New Hampshire after spending four years in Utah. After her husband's death, my sister Kathy met a fellow online and married again. I was glad for the two months they lived with me since I hadn't seen much of Kathy since I first married and moved to Utah many years before. Kathy had problems with her home dialysis and she was told she would need to live in a place with a permanent sewer, so they bought a house, lived in it a year or two, and then sold it for the truck and camper lifestyle. Somehow they did manage her home dialysis living in the camper. I never asked where they dumped the dialysis fluids.

It was July 2008 when I bought my one-level house. I was so happy with the attached garage and the automatic door opener. I had a coworker who was the age of my son Steven. We shared an office and talked about our families. I told him how much I liked my garage door opener and attached garage, and that it was the first time I had ever had one like that. He commented that he had always had one. No one told me that you should put your trash container in the garage for the winter, so there I was shoveling snow on the side of my house to store the trashcan. That was one thing I changed when someone suggested to me about putting the trashcan in the garage. I don't know why I hadn't thought of it myself, but for many years we had a detached garage, so the trash can was just outside.

I emailed Laddie about my renewed contact with my missionary and his wife after many years. My life continued, working, going to Church, spending time with children and grandchildren. Laddie was always there through email) over the years beginning in 1995. Then on March 9, 2011, I received an email from my dear friend and former coworker, Laddie. He informed me that his wife had passed away. He told me about a trip he was taking to visit his family in Indiana. On March 22, 2011, Laddie emailed me that he would let me know how his trip went when he got back. I waited, figuring maybe a weeklong trip, wondering when I would hear from him again. I had been single for eleven years. It seemed like a long time until April 9, when an email from him asked that I call him and that we could go to lunch sometime. Lunch didn't seem to work, so he invited me for Sunday dinner at his house. We spoke for over an hour on the phone, mostly about his recent experiences, his wife's passing, and his children at the hospital.

On April 10, I was ten minutes late. The meal was on the table, and Laddie and his granddaughter and her boyfriend were already at the table. I walked in, sat down, and the meal began. It felt strange; I hadn't seen Laddie in person for a number of years. His granddaughter and her boyfriend said very little. After the meal, Laddie pulled out some genealogy life stories he had written about deceased family members. He was showing me the collection of pictures in the back of each booklet. His granddaughter and her friend left, and we were sitting around the corner of the table from each other. Out of the blue, he leaned over and kissed me. That surprised me, coming so quickly. I knew his wife had cancer, but I thought nowadays people had more treatment options and recovered. Laddie, on the other hand, had known for months that his wife was dying. We caught up on each other's lives over the next few weeks, including a date to the Vernal Temple. On the ride that day, we asked each other many questions: "What's your favorite—" this or that.

Later, after agreeing that we wanted to get married, arrangements and plans seemed like too much to deal with since I was still working.

The prison had received some federal money, so they decided to require that anyone working with inmates had to wear a stab-proof vest. I found those to be very hot, especially during the previous August. Also, the last few years, the prison began requiring all caseworkers to certify on three different weapons. We didn't carry them on the job, but there were some we could have had access to at work. The previous year I did not pass the annual qualifying shoot, so I had to spend five full days practicing so I could qualify. But—Laddie came into my life, so now I considered retirement. I had just turned sixty-two, so if I were to retire, I could avoid the annual weapons test that was coming up. Also, I thought about the hot vests we were expected to wear all the time at work. I had several weeks of vacation time saved. I had planned to go to Florida with one of my sisters to visit our other two other sisters who lived there—one of them had a swimming pool. Our plane tickets were already bought.

I decided to retire, but that couldn't happen immediately. I needed to apply for Social Security. Laddie and I each owned a house, an hour apart. Which one would we live in? My children were all grown, but Carla and her husband were living with me. That was fine, but Adam would come back home occasionally to enjoy the use of the TV and the computer. I loved having them all around, but sons and sons-in-law don't always get along. What was I to do about that? Simple—I could move to Laddie's house when we got married.

I had a wedding date picked out and had paid for some deli food. We planned to be married in about a month. I couldn't get a definite commitment from some of my children whether they could be there to help with the food, which cost more than I had wanted. I didn't know what to do.

Chapter Twenty-Four

There is another incident that happened in that housing unit. One day I came to work as usual, and walked through the staff building and on down to the housing unit like I did every day. In this building, the inmates were almost always in their cells. I was confused when I saw about fifteen to twenty of the women in the entryway, sitting, standing, and hanging around. Rather than simply ask, "What are you doing here?" I instead asked, "What's this, a party and I wasn't invited?" Everyone started laughing, and several started talking at once.

I focused on one woman sitting near where I was standing, just inside the door. She said, "Yea, a party, a pee party!" After just a second or two, I understood, they were all called out and waiting for their turn to provide a urine sample. The inmate bathroom was near where they were all waiting. Another day I was working on assessments in my office by myself.

The officers had handcuffed one woman to the bar running along the bench that she was sitting on. She was there for quite a while, and at times would yell a variety of things, including that she wasn't going back to the infirmary. She had attempted suicide and had already spent a few days in the infirmary. She had been brought back to the housing unit, and something must have happened, so she was going back to the infirmary but was loudly protesting. Finally, the transport van came. She was a bit overweight and was refusing to go. She wouldn't walk and finally was lying on the floor. She wasn't fighting, she just lay limp and was not cooperating. Inmates don't get their own way; she *would* be taken to the transport van. At first, she was dragged a short distance. Then someone came with a long narrow flat board—not unlike a surfboard—with straps. She was rolled onto the board and strapped into place. She no longer yelled. She seemed to enjoy all the attention of the half dozen officers, both male and female.

On that board, they were able to get her out the door and near the van. The next problem was obvious. How would a person, lying straight, fit into a van that had all of its bench seats in place? Experienced officers had similar incidents happen and knew what to do. Someone called for an ambulance. Meanwhile, six or eight of us stood around talking. The inmate, still lying on the board, was thoroughly enjoying herself listening to the officers talking and joking with each other as they waited. She even laughed a bit. I guess this whole scene was more fun than sitting in her cell. Once the ambulance arrived, it was a simple matter of transferring her to the medical board that raises to the right height to conveniently get her into the vehicle. Away she left with no more noise. Her yelling had only occurred as she sat by herself in the lobby. She never seemed to mind that she was being moved once she was the center of attention.

Time passed. A mere three months went by when I was told I was being transferred again, over to another medium security women's unit. I went from my waterfall mural office to plain and stark and now to my John Wayne office. An inmate had painted a large horse with a large John Wayne. The other walls had famous quotes from John Wayne painted on them. There were two quotes I didn't care for so I had them painted over. Inmates keep asking if I am going to have John Wayne painted over with something more feminine. No, not for a while, maybe in a year I will. When I do, it will probably be an outdoor scene with a covered bridge.

As a teenager, I rode a school bus through a covered bridge every day to high school. My dad said that the reason the roof was on the bridge was so if a person was out in a horse and carriage and it started to rain or snow, they could wait in the covered bridge until the storm let up. That made sense to me, and now when I see a covered bridge I think of my dad. The women seem to like me as a caseworker. When I was transferred from the first women's unit after almost a year, the inmates made me four large thank-you cards, one from each section. I haven't actually counted the signatures, but it looks like almost every one of them must have signed it. I enjoy working at a job where people thank you for what you do—as well as getting paid.

I received a phone call from a detective in another state. She wanted to talk to an inmate. We arranged a time that she was to call back and I would have the inmate in my office. That didn't work. About ten minutes before the call was to come, the officers announced to everyone, "Lockdown, get to your cells." There had been a fight amongst three of the women, a relationship gone bad. So when the call came, I explained that our housing unit was in the middle of a lockdown. I told her that I would get the inmate to my office as soon as I could and we'd call her back. Fifteen minutes later, I was able to call her. Meanwhile, the ones in charge were questioning each of the inmates involved to find out what had happened and which of them should be moved to maximum security housing. I don't know how that turned out.

It was interesting listening to the long story as the woman answered questions about her husband that she hadn't seen in five years. It seems that he was a foreign person whom she had married. Later, she found papers with her name and social security number in his possession. Questioning him, she found out that he had used her in an attempt to become a citizen. They argued and finally split up. His culture was very domineering and she wasn't used to that. He wanted a divorce. She told him that was fine, but he would need to pay for it. He did some paperwork. She introduced him to another woman she knew. She said that woman knew he was still married. They got together and apparently got along for a few years. The detective told the inmate in my office that the money had never been paid for her divorce, so she was still married to the man. It seems that when the second woman no longer wanted the guy, she filed bigamy charges; hence, the detective was investigating. The inmate assured the detective that the woman knew he was married. The detective said that the bigamy charges would not hold up since the woman knew from the beginning that he was still married.

Another story I heard was when I was walking through the common area in one of the sections of the housing unit. I commented on the crocheting that a woman was doing. We started talking. She said how she was from a small town where the sheriff knew everyone. She had called the police three times when her husband had come home drunk and beaten her. They always acted like it was no big deal. The last time she called the police was after he came home drunk again and accused her of being unfaithful. She insisted to him that she had not been unfaithful.

He said he was going after that man to take care of him. Being afraid for the life of that man, she called the police. They got to the man's house first and stopped anything from happening. They arrested her husband for a day or two, due to an unlicensed car.

The police told her husband about his wife calling them. He went home and beat her up again. It was after that happened that she got a gun and shot him. She acted in self-defense so she wouldn't have to be beaten up and maybe killed in the future. Somehow, she was still found guilty and has now spent several years in prison with more to go. She said her defense attorney wasn't allowed to bring up in court the fact that her husband had four previous wives who were dead, and another wife missing. She had children with him and lived with him for eighteen years and now was in prison. It just didn't seem right. I told her that I enjoyed talking with her. As I left, she was in tears. She probably doesn't find many people in prison whom she can confide in.

Chapter TWENTY-FIVE

One Sunday night, Laddie said, "I don't want to wait, let's get married this weekend." I was still working four ten-hour days, Monday through Thursday, so I got off two hours early on Thursday and drove to Laddie's house and we were married in his front room. I hadn't said a word to my kids. I felt a bit guilty, but I reasoned that kids sometimes do that, go off and get married and then admit it later. My children were expecting a simple ceremony a month later. Instead, we called Laddie's LDS Bishop and he came over to Laddie's house and performed the service. The next day, I knew I should call my children and tell them what I had done. Again, Laddie came to my rescue, and before I knew it, he was on the phone telling one of my daughters who offered to tell the others. Soon the weekend was over and I headed back to my house so I could continue working four more weeks. Laddie came to my house Tuesday evenings and then we enjoyed the three-day weekends for the next month at his house.

Before I knew it, we were in Florida. I had gotten another plane ticket so Laddie went with me and my sister to visit our other two sisters. We were enjoying their swimming pool, when I started thinking about some things. I was already retired, so I could go home and collect the vacation pay that I had coming. Then life would be good, newly married, and receiving social security and my state retirement with the time to do what we wanted.

Six months later, I analyzed our routines. We were both retired, and Laddie fixed breakfast. I took care of the dishes. We went to the Temple twice a month. He was the high priest's group leader in our ward and I taught a primary class. He did his home teaching; I had visiting teaching. Errands included the bank, grocery store, and Deseret Industries (a thrift store), with Church on Sunday. He likes toy fire trucks and books; for me, it was Barbies that I crocheted dresses for. Then we would find a place for lunch to use a buy-one/get-one free coupon. We also listened to conservative talk shows on the radio and news on TV. I am glad that when Laddie reads, it is out loud; I knit or crochet and listen. Often he reads scriptures and then historical fiction. Our favorite errands include visiting our children.

Now many months later, a grandson, his wife, and son moved in and stayed a year. Then there were other grandchildren in and out. One time that included two great-grandchildren. Currently, we have two grandsons and their cousin, a granddaughter, living with us. I do appreciate this home we have now after living in Laddie's multilevel house for a year. When we moved in, with three bedrooms on the main level, I designated two of them as offices, one for me and one for Laddie. After all, we both had been caseworkers for a lot of years and we always had offices. We have the main level with the grandchildren downstairs. Laddie recently got a sign saying "Bunkhouse" that he installed over the stairs as one goes downstairs.

Then our lives took a drastic turn that lasted for over a year. First, Laddie was diagnosed as needing a sleep apnea machine. There were delays in actually getting the machine. He called several times, but still waited. Then he began having difficulty swallowing. He was eating less and started losing weight. For Labor Day weekend, he invited his kids, who lived nearby, to a backyard meal. Being diabetic, Laddie took his insulin as usual, but only took a bite or two and went back to the house feeling really bad. One of his kids checked his blood sugar and it was not far from being fatal. After a quick try with some honey in a spoon, we found that was too thick for his swallowing issue, so we got him into the car and drove to the nearest emergency room. Three days later, Laddie came home with a feeding tube going through his nose and down into his stomach. He felt a lot better and had to get used to the feeding tube taped to his cheek.

We were referred to an ear, nose, and throat doctor who poked in his throat a few times and said that the muscles on the left side of his tongue and throat didn't seem to be working and recommended that we see a neurologist. The neurologist said it could be a stroke or something called myasthenia gravis (MG). A brain scan showed no evidence of a stroke. For MG, Laddie was prescribed Pyridostigmine, also called Mestinon.

After Laddie was on that medication for only one day, I received a call from the doctor, asking how he was doing with his swallowing. I explained that he was on the feeding tube, but he no longer talked like he had a swollen tongue. After that phone call, I started thinking that the doctor must have expected fairly quick results from the medication. As a result, I decided to do what I had seen the speech therapist do, I gave Laddie very small bits from a fruit cocktail cup. That seemed to work okay, so Laddie began to eat more, still with the feeding tube in. First, he ate only soft foods, then for about a week he ate foods he wanted. The next swallow test wasn't so good. Two weeks later Laddie contracted pneumonia, probably due to food going into the lungs.

On September 1, Laddie went into the hospital. A ventilation tube was put down his throat to help with breathing. That required sedation, which was administered. After a few days, his sedation amount was lessened and he was given Ativan as needed (a common medication to help a person relax). Laddie seemed like he was sedated most of the time. The nurses kept telling me that he hadn't received any sedation, just the Ativan. The ventilator tube that went down his throat was removed when the tracheostomy was done, putting a smaller tube in a hole in his neck, rather than the larger one down his throat. At the time of the surgery Laddie was still under the influence of the Ativan overdose. I expressed my frustrations to Laddie's daughter, that Laddie could not even squeeze a person's hand when he appeared to be awake, and that the nurses claimed they were only giving him Ativan and no sedation. She said she had read on the Internet that a person with myasthenia gravis should not have Ativan. Immediately I printed that out from more than one source. When I showed that to the hospital, they stopped the Ativan.

The next day, Laddie was wide awake and alert with a trach tube inserted into his neck. With his MG, a normal dose of Ativan had been like an overdose to him. That same day, Laddie was sent in an ambulance to a skilled nursing facility. He arrived bleeding from his mouth. It was a really good thing that he was wide awake and alert that day, so the doctors were able to ask if he felt nauseated. They knew the two-day old trach surgery could be bleeding on the inside, but they didn't know if blood was also coming from the stomach. Laddie was alert and able to shake his head to say "no" since a person cannot talk with a trach in the neck.

Laddie had been flat on his back for just over two weeks, so his muscle tone was gone. I had never felt leg and arm muscles that were completely like Jell-O. That meant physical therapy and occupational therapy, which he began. Laddie was then moved to a regular nursing home where his therapy continued. Surgery was done to move the feeding tube from the nose directly into the stomach. The wrong anesthesia was used—one that affected Laddie's muscles receptors, which were already diminished by his MG. However, that wore off in one day and Laddie was able to walk as well as he had the day before that surgery. Three months at that care center ended on January 23. So, from September 1 until January 23. Laddie had been in either a hospital or a care center. My schedule was to visit and spend time with him every day from 9:00 a.m. till about 6:00 p.m., which I had done the entire time. He would sleep or go for therapy, or we would read together, and I crocheted a lot. At the hospitals, I could buy meals, but the care center gave me two free meals a day.

Back in July and August, I had learned to take care of a feeding tube, but on January 23, I had to take care of his trach at home. He still used a wheelchair a lot. That meant getting up in the night and helping him from the hospital bed to the bathroom and back to bed. Then there were prescriptions to fill and setting up his pills in the weekly trays. Still having the feeding tube, it was necessary to crush the pills and use a syringe to administer the pill water into the feed tube. I learned how to give him his insulin shots, which he had been doing for many years. The nurses had done that in the hospitals and care center, but now I did it, along with the suctioning and cleaning of the trach.

Needless to say, I learned a lot and kept busy those two months that Laddie was home, but I was finally able to start him on some food supplements, Digestacure-AutoimmuneX, that I found on the Internet. I previously ordered them, but they didn't arrive until after Laddie was hospitalized on September 1. Those supplements were developed over fifteen years, as a doctor worked on finding something for anyone with any autoimmune disease. It was very frustrating to me; I asked at every hospital and care center that Laddie was in if I could bring the food supplements in to give him. The answer was always no. But now Laddie was home and he began receiving those food supplements.

Another part of Laddie's treatment for his myasthenia gravis was plasmapheresis. He had that blood filtering done several times, mid-August, mid-September, the end of December, and the first of March.

Laddie had been through seven months of having a feeding tube and watching food commercials on TV, and five months with a trach and not being able to talk. He became discouraged and depressed, so I took him to a doctor about the depression. He was prescribed Celexa, one and a half pills each evening. Then I started noticing agitation and confusion. He was not able to use his cell phone. Again, searching the Internet, I found that a person with myasthenia gravis should not have Celexa, but it could only be reduced week by week, which I did.

After two months at home and having his food supplements, Laddie developed a fever. We went to the hospital on March 22. They found that a healed-over bedsore was still infected. Another surgery was done to remove his tailbone, which a person doesn't need anyway. When Laddie went back to the hospital on March 22, I gave intake a copy of Laddie's medications, which still included the last half a pill a day of the Celexa. Celexa was being administered in the evening. I visited during the day and wasn't aware of any problems. It was three weeks until a nurse commented to me that sometimes at night Laddie was agitated. When I heard that, I knew—we checked what medications the hospital was giving him. They had ignored my list of his meds and looked on their computer for the last doctor's orders and found the one and a half pills of Celexa per day that he was originally prescribed. I immediately spoke to the doctor. At first he felt challenged and said that he had been to medical school and that I shouldn't believe everything that I found on the Internet. After a few days, I had the nurse check their records and found that the doctor had begun reducing the amount of Celexa. Poor Laddie with his MG, first those weeks of overdosing on Celexa at home, and then the same thing happening in the hospital.

Since Laddie's infection was in the bone, it required a long term antibiotic that he received in the hospital and in the next care facility he went to until May 20. Medicare would not pay for that antibiotic to be administered at home—maybe because it was through an IV into the vein. One of the hospitals and one of the care facilities had been an hour away from where we lived, so I packed some of my clothes and went first for one month and then later for two months and stayed with Adam, who owned his own home. From there, I was able to still visit Laddie every day and still see more of my grown children in the evenings than I had been able to for quite a while.

Back home on May 20, Laddie was able to have the Digestacure-AutoimmuneX again, and by then we knew about a possible surgery that Laddie was to have had on March 24 (except that he went back in the hospital on March 22).

At least three times, a tiny camera on a cord had been put down Laddie's throat. The first time, the left side of his throat didn't work very well and the right side didn't work at all. The next two times the left side worked fine and the right side still didn't work at all. The conclusion was that during his pneumonia the previous September, the right side had been permanently damaged when the ventilator tube had been inserted. That was one possible side effect, when his breathing was at risk and they thought he needed the ventilator tube.

The throat surgery was finally done on June 15; it involved putting a spacer (maybe a type of sponge or something) in the right side of Laddie's throat to move the right side, non-working vocal folds over, closer to center to prevent food or liquids from entering the lungs. Within a week, both the trach and the feeding tube were removed. Laddie was very happy to be able to eat and talk again. We tried every new food or sandwich that he could remember from the commercials, and he gave up the clipboard and writing notes as he had done for so long now that he could talk again. Laddie had a muscle/nerve test done and was told that he had no signs of any myasthenia gravis. The current medical community doesn't acknowledge any cure for myasthenia gravis. Either the food supplements cured his MG, or, as the doctors prefer to say, it must have been a mini-stroke that just didn't show up in the brain scan, which was given more than once.

Having followed my husband's medical condition the whole year, I know he had reactions to the Ativan, the particular type of anesthesia, and the Celexa just as a person with myasthenia gravis would have. I would recommend the Digestacure-AutoimmuneX to anyone with any autoimmune disease, since I believe it really helped my husband.

Laddie and I are very grateful to all the family members and friends who have supported us throughout this last year. Laddie and I have gotten back to our regular lives, attending to Church, still doing errands with a few more online, still going out to eat, including our $3 each senior citizen lunches. Laddie had just finished writing his book, *Doing Time at the Utah*

State Prison, before this last year of medical problems. It can be found amazon.com.

The way I remember it, about two years before I retired and married him, I mentioned to him that I was writing about my experiences working in the prison. He thought that was a good idea and did the same, and being the storyteller he is, he came up with many more pages than I did. Now finishing mine, I can return to my favorite hobbies: genealogy, knitting, and crocheting.

Eileen Preutt

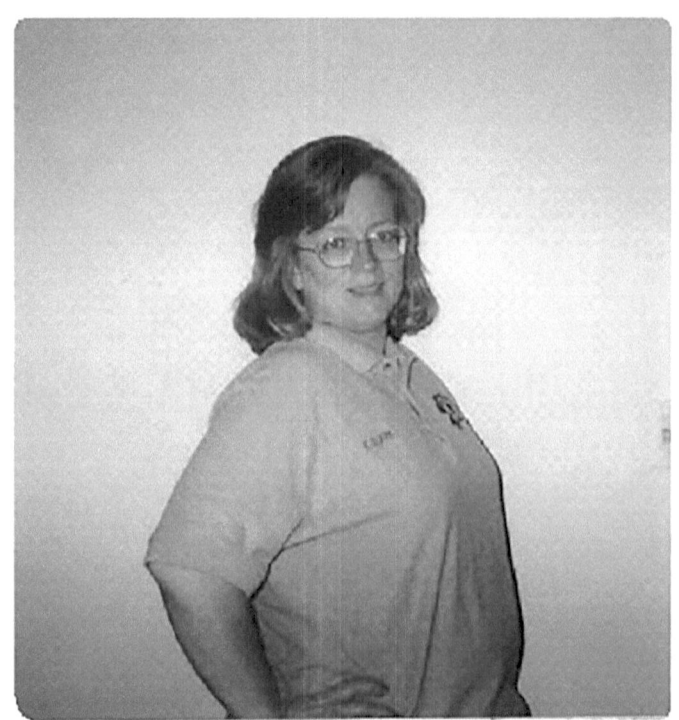

Book Review by Jonah Meyer

"My two lives seemed so different. At home I cooked, cleaned, did laundry. Work was a different feeling. I felt important, writing reports, recommendations to the Board of Pardons and Parole."

Pruett, married to the man she loved and met through her involvement with The Church of Jesus Christ of Latter-Day Saints, was a busy and dedicated mom, raising no less than eight children. Having joined the Church at age thirteen, she often dreamed of the day she would attend Brigham Young University in Utah, in some ways a world away from the small rural New Hampshire town where she grew up. In February of 1968, she met Don. Their first date was a movie date, seeing The Graduate. There's a good reason the idiom "The rest, as they say, is history" is cliché, as this certainly applies in the life of the author of this absorbing, comprehensive memoir.

The reader meets Laddie, who for many years worked alongside Pruett in her role of inmate caseworker with the prison system, where she was responsible for a wide array of duties from housing assessment to prison intake to her primary work as caseload manager. She met regularly with the inmates, assessed through deep-dive research if and when any were to be recommended for parole, and reported her findings to her higher-ups. Throughout the book, Pruett shares anecdote after anecdote from her career working with both the inmates and her colleagues. The relationships she established—especially with those behind bars—are eye-opening and not necessarily what one might imagine. Sometimes unsettling, sometimes extremely humorous, the reader is treated to an "insider's look" into the realities of work as a member of the prison staff.

This memoir easily stands out as being unique from page one to the end. It describes how the author learns to navigate her "two worlds" of home life—rearing her beautiful children and deep involvement with the Church—versus the career where she "truly felt free." The chapters themselves alternate between these two realities. For example, as readers learn of the many struggles and victories in one setting, many of the same issues are mirrored in the other. Pruett's choice to tell her story in this manner is perhaps its greatest strength.

Additionally, the author's voice is exceedingly down-to-earth, humble, and frank. Here is a woman who has accomplished so much good in terms of helping other people in ways both large and small and is now simply telling her story. Completely absent of any pretense, she comes across as having a laid-back conversation with the reader. This is quite refreshing, and in the process, one becomes intimately familiar with the intricacies of learning how the author eventually acquired confidence working in such close proximity with men who have committed any number of crimes—including in some cases the unimaginable acts of murder and rape.

Pruett completed her degree in childhood development and family relations, with a minor in mathematics, through a combination of home study and night classes. In retirement, she now has more time and energies to devote to her true, cherished passions. Among these are genealogical research, connecting the dots to an ever-increasing family tree record through individual, intriguing stories of relatives, and preserving visual artifacts (such as photographs and the like). Her memoir is a well-written record of a fascinating career and a life well-lived.

RECOMMENDED by the US Review

www.ingramcontent.com/pod-product-compliance
Lightning Source LLC
Chambersburg PA
CBHW030157100526
44592CB00009B/325